A Devotional

The River Narrows
SEEING THE LORD'S HAND IN EVERYDAY LIFE

by: Max Floyd

Copyright © 2014 Max Floyd

All rights reserved

Publisher: rgjbooks

Winston Salem, NC

rgjbooks@gmail.com

rgjbooks.blogspot.com

Table of Contents   Pg

The Fall

Week 1
On Every Corner	1
Wasted Gas, Wasted Time	4
Treasure of Stone	7
Power Washed Life	11

Week 2
The Hunger Games	15
Look Before You Reach	19
Good Soil	23
Black Friday and the Deal of a Lifetime	26

Week 3
Battle for the Mind	30
Old Tree in the Middle of the Yard	33
The Perfect Gift	36
An Oil Change	40

Week 4
Friendships Over the Years	44
Inside Out, New Year's Resolution	48
Moving Water or Frozen Pipes	52
Power Lines that Never Go Down	56

Week 5
Every Waking Second	60
The Fog	64
Irrigation Plans	67
The Mantle	71

Week 6
Voices	75
Diamonds on the Street	80
The Tin Man	84
A Place in Line, A Place at Home	88

Week 7
Scales in Our Lives	93
What I Thought Was Good, Was Bad	97
Only When It Works For Me	100
Life Coins	105

Week 8
Freezing Rain	109
Hot and Cold	113
The Baton	117
Putting Off to Put On	121

Week 9
Only One Person for the Job	125
Spiritual Fitness	129
My Truck	131
Birthdays	133

The Winter

Week 10
Generation iY	136
Making a Withdrawal	138
In the Beloved	141
White as Snow	145

Week 11
Pre-Emergent 148
Man's Best Friend 151
Getting Away 153
Roots Run Deep 157

Week 12
Audit Joy 162
Awake at the Wheel 165
One Shining Life 168
Render Unto Caesar 171

Week 13
90 Mile Per Arm 175
The Mirror 178
He's My Friend 182
The Walking Dead 185

Week 14
Run and Not Be Weary 188
Never Full 191
Never Out of Range 194
Out of the Garage, Made New 197

Week 15
Seemingly Safe, Unbearably Hot 202
Trust 206
He Is There and He Is Not Silent 210
The River Narrows 214

Week 16
Work Until It Is Finished	219
Words or Silence?	224
Teacher We Know, Teachers We Are	228
Runaway Ramp	232

Week 17
Valentine's Day Hearts	237
One Umbrella, One Life	241
Two Rescues	245
Pull the Tarps	249

Week 18
The Wrong Finish Line	252
When Practice Ends	256
It is Finished	260
The Lord is Faithful	263

Forward/Acknowledgements

In the spring of 2012, my son, a student at Wake Forest University was meeting with a campus ministry intern and several students for bible study on campus. This young intern was pouring into these young men's lives and I could not wait to someday meet this gentleman who was keeping alive the spiritual priorities of students all across campus. When we finally did meet, we opened up our home to his band of brothers not knowing what would eventually become commonplace in our household. Week after week, anywhere from seven to fifteen young men would walk through our doors eagerly anticipating the relational and wise words of their mentor. In time, as I was invited to listen in and then eventually open in prayer, something began anew in my heart. I began to love and appreciate these guys.

As life sometimes does, paths change directions. This was the case with this intern. Full time ministry came calling and his first step was a move to advanced schooling in seminary. With this prerequisite, there had to be a stepping off point for what was currently taking place in his life, his bible study commitments on campus. Since our home was open and I was interested, I agreed to continue the study for the guys, the band of brothers. Week after week, the guys continued to show up at the door eager to have some of my wife's wonderful cooking and hear from God's word. Month after month, this continued with only summer break chopping up the meeting times.

In order to move the guys forward in their walks with their God, one evening I issued a challenge. I challenged the guys to walk with their God for 100 straight days. I asked them to take time out of every day for the next 100 days to be with their God in some way. I told them that I would like them to do a devotional every day. Later on that evening, I received an email from one of the guys who was in attendance. The note went something like this, "Dear Mr. Floyd. I would like to take part in this 100 day challenge. However, I do not know what a devotional is. Would you please help me understand what this means to have one each day?" I replied back, "Friend, not to worry. I will write one for you and the guys every day for the next 100 days. You read along and we will grow together."

For 100 straight days, I wrote a devotional for the band of brothers. Every evening before midnight or soon thereafter, I would complete the day's devotional. On Saturdays and Sundays I would write in the mornings or early afternoons. If I was away at tournaments or conferences, I would make sure that I would find time to do their devotional. It was a rich time. Each day I would look for God's handiwork and craft what I observed or experienced into words which the guys would understand. After 100 days we completed the challenge but that did not last for long. The fall eventually came around and the need for a biweekly devotional surfaced.

This past fall we set out once again on another devotional journey. Through God's grace, we completed the Fall/Winter 40. This that you are about to open is a collection of 72 of the 140 devotionals that were originally written. Lord willing, I will continue to write and volume II will arrive someday soon. As I challenged the guys those many months ago, may you also find time each day to be with your God. May this series of devotionals, in some way, nourish your mind, your hearts and your souls to long after your Maker who loves you more than we can ever imagine. As you will read many times in the following pages, 'Draw near to God and He will draw near to you.'

Sincerely,

Max Floyd

Dedication

To the guys who have come by our house, eaten my wife's wonderful cooking, listened to my words and read my impressions of God's moment by moment presence in our lives. Thank you for allowing my wife and I into your world. It has been a real privilege and joy to meet you and to hopefully encourage you in some way. May the words in this collection not only bring remembrance of the original email devotionals but may these words spur you on to more love for our Lord and continued good deeds in the world around you. Our Lord desires for you to know Him and walk with Him. As I will look and continue to see His fingerprints, may you also experience His presence as you open each chapter of your ever evolving life story. You have made a difference in our lives. May you now be a blessing in the lives of countless others.

Max

On Every Corner

My wife's van just hit 251,600 miles. After getting behind the wheel a few weeks back on a drive to Greensboro, I finally admitted that we needed a change. Several situations with the van have forced me to rethink my denial mindset that I had been carrying for quite some time. First of all, the air conditioning unit is broken. With another hot summer just around the corner, this is a very important yet pricey fix. Second, the front wheel alignment and bearings are showing significant vibration. This of course is not just an annoyance but a safety issue. Then there are several other issues that will need the investment of money very soon as well. The key to the ignition will not go back into the ignition if taken out, the back two tires are quite worn and the dashboard light controls are broke. As you can see, it is time for a new car. We started looking yesterday. Two cars seemed to come to the surface. We started looking at the Toyota Highlander and the Honda Pilot. It has been an enjoyable hunt filled with dozens of web searches, two different dealership visits and finally a test drive. We are still in the process and should me making a decision shortly.

However, something interesting has happened during this search. Something has happened that I did not notice just a couple days ago. What is new is this; before I started looking for a new Highlander or Pilot, I did not notice them at all on the road. I did not notice them when I was driving to work, when going to the store, when going to ballgames, when going to the ball fields, when going to friends' houses, when getting gas or when I was going to the bank. Before I started looking for a Highlander or Pilot, I had no idea that they were even on the road with me. Now that I am looking for them, everything has changed. Now that I am looking for a Highlander/Pilot I now see them on every corner. I see them on the way to work. I see them on the way to the store, on the way to the fields, on the way to the mall. I see them everywhere. What has changed? Were they not there before? Were they not right next to me on the roads before? Have they all of a sudden surfaced into my life? Or, have they been there all along? Have they been there but I just did not notice? You see, it is true, they have been there all along. I just was not looking. I was not looking for their presence in my life. All along, they were right next to me, going in front of me, coming behind me, crossing my path in every possible direction. They have been there all along. I was just not looking for them.

Look around. Something has been going on in your life for quite some time now. Something, no someone, has been coming into your path every day, every moment, in every possible location, and in every possible situation. We just have missed seeing Him, that's all. You see the Lord Jesus is all around your life and is calling you. He is calling you to Himself, for you to acknowledge Him, for you to love Him, for you to glorify Him, for you to follow Him. Will you look up and see his handiwork? Will you look across the intersection and see His wonderful works? Will you see His working in every subject matter, in every relationship, in every trial, in every victory, in every disappointment or failure? You see, He has been there and will continue to be there all along. You see, He is our ever present help in trouble, in distress, in confusion and in life. Begin to look for Him as you start, go through and finish your day. Look for Him as you open the scriptures each day. Begin to look for Him as you see the wonders of His creation. Begin to look for Him as you speak to Him in prayer. Begin to look for Him everywhere. He is there. Just like those Highlanders and Pilots, He has always been there all along. He is there for you. You just have to open your eyes.

He loves you and wants to be at the center of your life. Acknowledge Him and follow Him today and every day. If you do, I promise, no He promises, to never leave you nor forsake you.

Some scriptures to ponder include:

Hebrews 11:6 "But without faith it is impossible to please Him, for he who comes to God must believe that He exists, and that He is a rewarder of those who diligently see Him."

Psalm 8:3 "When I consider Your heavens, the work of your fingers, the moon and the stars, which you have ordained, what is man that you are mindful of him and the son of man that You visit him?"

James 1:25 "But he who looks into the perfect law of liberty and continues in it, and is not a forgetful hearer but a doer of the word, this one will be blessed in what he does."

Keep seeking for Him. Keep looking for Him. Keep acknowledging Him. He can be found. He is there. He has spoken and will speak life words to you if you only let Him.

Scripture reading: Psalm 139

Draw near to God and He will draw near to you.

Wasted Gas, Wasted Time

Saturday, as with many households across our land, is a work day. Since most everyone is busy during the week, one usually does not have the necessary time to get all of the house chores and yard work done. There is a tendency for things to pile up. However, as Saturday arrives, hope for order is rekindled once again. One Saturday a while back was one of those work days for me. I woke up early and made plans to make a big dent in the to-do list. I had tasks that needed to be done and only one day in which to do them. I knew that the evening would be here before I knew it so I got after it first thing Saturday morning.

The day started out wonderfully. In just two hours I was able to remove some old window blinds in a room and then install brackets along with three additional new sets of blinds. I was feeling pretty confident about getting everything done until I needed to make a run to Lowes Home Improvement. Everything was fine until I started down the road toward Lowes. I needed to replace three sidewall AC/Heating vents in two rooms so a quick run to the store was necessary. I thought I knew what I wanted and headed out the door aiming to get the items that I needed. I planned on returning quickly to do the rest of the house and yard work. As it turned out, because of the decisions that I made in preparation, I spent the rest of the day in just one room only achieving about 30% of a day which I had planned.

This is what happened which set me up for a day which did not reach anywhere close to the potential I set out to achieve. First of all, I went to Lowes without a correct plan. I went to Lowes and purchased the AC/heat registers that I needed but found out

4

once I got home that what I had bought would not fit. I had purchased floor registers instead of side wall register vents. So, after driving 20 minutes to Lowes and 20 minutes back, I now had to jump back into the truck for another trip to Lowes to return and exchange the poorly chosen vents. After another hour of driving and waiting in line to exchange the wrongly purchased items, I finally returned home to face the next obstacle on the home chore list. As it turned out, the afternoon continued to go in a poor direction. I continued down the to-do list only to discover time and time again that I did not have the proper tools and needed supplies. What should have been a list of quick fixes, turned into a full day of wasting gas and wasting time.

In sum, the whole day could have reached its potential if I only would have done it right the first time. If I would have looked at what was truly needed; if I would have assembled the right tools and supplies; if I would have done it right the first time, I would not have had to push the reset button. If I would have just taken my time, surveyed the scene and drawn upon the available resources, I would have had success the first time. Instead, I had to start all over, go all the way back to the beginning and do it all over again. I wasted gas and wasted time because I failed to do it right the first time.

This is exactly how life is. Oftentimes we want to head down a path of life without looking at the directions, surveying the scene and using the proper tools. We run out the door of life without a clear plan and a clear set of directions set before us. In essence, we want to do it our own way. We oftentimes neglect the right path which has been made known to us and we forge ahead on our own only to find out what I found out that Saturday morning. We find out that we have been just wasting gas and wasting time. We have to start all over again.

5

My desire for you is not to do in life what I did that day. My desire for you is for you to do it right the first time. If we do not follow the path of righteousness which the good Lord has set before us, it will eventually fall apart. When that happens, we eventually find that we must start all over again, back at the beginning. On our walk back to the beginning oftentimes we wonder what life could have been like if we just would have stayed on the right course the first time around.

Living a life with God at the center is the right path. Living a life where you think of the Lord, talk to the Lord and read the words of the Lord is the correct direction. So as you get ready to start another chapter in your life, I urge you to remember my wasted trip to Lowes and to apply it to your life. Walk with the Lord now, get to know Him now, serve Him with all your heart now for in so doing you will never have to start all over again. A daily walk with the Lord is true life and true peace. A daily moment by moment relationship conversing with the Lord God Almighty is true joy. Don't miss it. However, one quick thing; I have had to hit the reset button in my life myself.

I have had to start over. Yes, I have burned a lot of gas and wasted time myself but one thing is for sure. The Lord took me back every time and He will do the same even if you have made a poor choice trip to Lowes.

Scripture reading: Proverbs 3: 5, 6; Jeremiah 17:5-8

Draw near to God and He will draw near to you.

6

Treasure of Stone

Sometimes you find treasure in the most unlikely places. A few days back, I got to see it for myself. I pulled up to a job site on a big construction project and just off the path to the site, laying there mixed in with piles of fill dirt, were dozens of rocks. These rocks were not just normal everyday rocks; these had a very unique shape. As I moved closer to get a closer view of the rocks, I noticed that they were all about the same size and shape. From what I could see they were old cobblestones. Possibly at one time, this pile of stones was the foundation for a road laid underneath that area years ago. Trees, mud and rotting wood were now covering these stones but many were poking up through the surface so I continued with my exploration of the site.

As I was now in the midst of the dirt pile I looked and noticed that these were perfectly cut old blocks of stone. Once this thought became clearer in my mind I became very excited. After getting the go ahead to get them, I immediately started gathering some of these mementos from a time gone by. I needed to get them soon as they were scheduled to be loaded into dump trucks heading for a landfill. As I hovered over these stones, I picked the first one up, knocked off a large chunk of dirt and lifted it up to get a better view of its shape. It was light brown, about one foot across, six inches tall and about eight to ten inches deep. From a chip on one of the corners, the rock looked like it was some kind of granite because of the pieces of white quartz-like speckles shining throughout.

As I gazed excitedly at the new found treasure in my hands, I wondered what the story was of this old cobblestone dump site. Was it an old road laid stone by stone by a workman years

7

ago? Or, was this area just a collection of randomly strewn stones cast away into a depression on the side of a hill? Regardless of the story which someday I hope to ascertain, I did know one thing for sure. Each one of these stones at one time or another was hewn out of a large piece of rock. At one time, each one of these stones were hand crafted chipped and chiseled at just the right angle, just the right size, all to meet the street layer's wishes. At one time, this piece of stone was intentionally made for a purpose, a needed purpose, an important purpose.

As I took the first stone and laid it into my truck, I knew that I had a wonderful find on my hands. From this point on I will now be able to enjoy the choice, the work and the crafting of a quarryman from a time gone by. Now in my yard, I will be able to see the results of a person who took a big portion of his time to create a stone which would one day meet a need. Now, from this day forward, I will be able to see firsthand the rebirth of a rock which at one time had a purpose, one time had a special place, one time had a job to do in order to make the world a better place. Yesterday, I saw them, took them and will shortly put them in a role which will be seen and enjoyed by many for hopefully years to come.

The word of God speaks of this very same discovery. Like myself pulling to a construction site yesterday, there is a hillside of human stones hewn out of our Creators mind shaped exactly how the He wanted. Just like my view to an area off the side of the road, there is also an area where fine stones have been laid waiting just beneath the surface waiting to spring forth. As you know, these stones are His children. God's thoughts, (His word), talks about how we, like the stone worker, are a result of His handiwork. It talks about how we are His own creation and built

8

for a purpose in the world. We are his workmanship. Ephesians 2:10 says "For we are His workmanship, created in Christ Jesus for good works, which God prepared beforehand that we should walk in them."

When you personally believe that the Lord Jesus died for your sins and was raised on the third day, washing away your sins, giving you eternal life, you are God's stone, a Christian. When you personally trust in the Lord Jesus Christ for not only life after death but for everyday life now, you are God's stone, a Christian. When you walk with Him day by day, confessing your sins when they become apparent, and thanking Him for His blessings, you are God's stone, a Christian. You are a stone of His making, a stone of His choice, a stone which He has placed on the hillside of our world. We are not to stay in the dirt pile waiting to be hauled off to some thankless, landfill, but we are to make ourselves available for the Master's work which He has prepared for us to do in advance. Some of you may be placed in a road building a pathway for others to enjoy. Others may be in a wall surrounding a village thus protecting the inhabitants. And still others may be inside a work of art for others to see and enjoy.

We all have a purpose. We all have a place. Leave the pile on the side of the road and find your place. We need you. The world needs you. If you are steadily acknowledging the Lord as your Creator and following the Lord as your stone fashioner, you will experience life as it was meant to be experienced.

Have a great day. Look around for some stones who might need to get back into the game. Look around for some stones who might need some mud knocked off. Look around for an opportunity for yourselves to fill a gap. I can't wait to see it.

Scripture reading: Matthew 5:16

Draw near to God and He will draw near to you.

Power Washed Life

Several mornings back I got up to do some exterior paver and sidewalk work. Since a regular garden hose has only limited psi (pressure), I had to break out the power washer from the shed. The front porch cobblestones needed some clean up but as I quickly found out the concrete steps leading up to the front door was caked in black summer mold as well. After checking the oil and topping off the gas tank with some fuel, I went to work. It was truly amazing the transformation which I observed. Of our 17 years or so in our home, I do not remember power washing the front steps. You can imagine the layers which needed to be cleared.

I choked the engine, turned the machine to run and cranked it up. With the water running full steam and the engine doing its job, I began blasting the stones and concrete steps. At first the task seemed too long and cumbersome. There were dozens of square feet to cover and the wand only covered a few inches at a time. Nevertheless, I stuck to the task and slowly but surely removed the caked black mold from days gone by. The power of the wand instantly blew past the sludge going to the pure original concrete. The ugly covering from years of weathering and dampness came off showing a newness and cleanness that I never knew was possible. As I applied the power wash, I called to my wife asking her to see the change. It was exciting. It was exciting in that at one time our steps were a stained covering now they were as new. Once they were as crimson now they were as white as snow.

As I power washed the steps that morning, I am reminded of a power washing which took place in my life during my first year in college. A friend took the time at Arizona State University to

11

share with me the fact that my front steps, my back deck as well as every room in my life were stained with sin. Though I tried to put up a clean look, my life was still characterized by no faith, no spiritual life, no desire to do God's will, no desire to love others, no desire to walk holy before my Maker. As many of you know, this was just the evidence that I had never had become a new creation. I had never at a specific time and date believed on the Lord Jesus Christ for the forgiveness of my sin which dominated my life. I had never become a new creation. I had never had my sins power washed away, cast away as far as the east from the west, never to be remembered any more.

So, in the quiet of my residence hall, on the 4th floor of Palo Verde West on the campus of Arizona State University, I asked Jesus Christ into my life. I received Him as my Lord and Savior and claimed His forgiveness of all of my sins that I have ever committed and will ever commit in the future. At that very moment, Jesus, because of the shedding of His blood on the cross, took my sins and washed them away. From that point on I was a new man. I was clean. The ugly mold was gone forever lost in the sea of forgiveness.

As I have grown to understand over the years, God has spoken on this very topic. II Corinthians 5:17 says "Therefore, if anyone is in Christ, he is a new creation; the old has gone, the new has come."

And Isaiah 1:18 says "Come now, let us reason together," says the Lord. "Though your sins are like scarlet, they shall be as white as snow; though they are red as crimson, they shall be like wool."

And John 1:12 "Yet to all who received him, to those who believed in his name, he gave the right to become children of God."

12

You see, we are all born with steps stained in mold and all we do until we meet the Lord is to add to it. We may add a new color to the mold. We may name the mold something else. We may even blame the mold that is evident on our family history, our culture or even our personality. Nevertheless, no matter how you look at it, it is sin that is in our way to eternal life with the Lord and an abundant life in the here and now.

So I ask you all this day, what is the condition of your steps? Are they as white as snow? Or like my steps were that morning a few days back and my life those years ago in Arizona, are they as crimson? Are they getting in the way of the life that the good Lord would like to give you? Ask Him to do His work today. Ask Him to apply the power of the life cleansing death, burial and resurrection of the Lord Jesus. If you do, I do promise, our Lord promises, that you will be a new creation. You will have eternal life, clean before the Lord, primed and ready to attack life with the Almighty right by your side. Trust Him today. It is a power washing to the core that we all need. First John says "He who has the Son has life and he who does not have the Son does not have life." Choose the Son this day. He changed my life and I know He will change yours.

I will be praying for you all this very day. Lots of mold threatens to stain and cover our lives every day. As you know, there is someone who can help you in this battle. He is there and He is not silent. He wants to show you life as it is supposed to be lived. Read what He says daily.

13

Speak to Him throughout the day. Confess your sins as the mold hits the steps. And finally gather together as often as you can with those who believe and will encourage a life in the Lord.

Scripture reading: II Corinthians 13:5

Draw near to God and He will draw near to you.

The Hunger Games

A couple weeks back I was asked to lead the games section of our church wide picnic. My job was to come up with a series of games for the entire congregation to enjoy. In preparation I knew that there would be participants ranging from 10 years old to almost 70. It was a challenging task but one which I eagerly accepted. As it turned out, we did a series of games lasting close to one hour and fifteen minutes. Many of the games involved the crowning of an individual champion. Other games ended when a whole team received the victor's crown. Some of the games pitted whit's and focus. Other games forced speed and athleticism to surface. At the end of the day, I do believe all who participated had a good time and enjoyed the opportunity to engage in some healthy competition. No one's income was on the line. No one's health was put in jeopardy. No one's life was held in the balance. The games which we played yesterday were nowhere close to the Hunger Games.

"May the odds be ever in your favor" is the phrase used over and over in the movie which took our country by storm a few years back. The title of the movie is "The Hunger Games." Though hunger was a periodic concern for Katniss Everdeen and the other key characters, surviving arrows, swords and weapons of other contestants was. Though food was what they needed to hunger for from time to time, they really needed to hunger for keeping alive. Every contestant in the hunger games was pitted against the other in a competition which would crown only one champion. Once the hunger games were over, all others would have died. Each would have survived one on one combats with all others entitling them to a life time of privilege. If one would win, he or she would no longer have to hunger for food, friendship or for life itself. They would be filled.

15

Much like the church games that I conducted the other day and to an extent the Hunger Games of Hollywood, all who play in the game of life do hunger after certain things. At the church picnic contestants were hungering after the title of picnic champion. In the "Hunger Games" story and movie, contestants were hungering after survival of life itself. We all hunger after things which are presented to us each and every day. Some of them are noble. Some of them are not so noble. Some of them are good for us. Some of them are not so good for us.

The Lord God almighty is the creator of life. The ever-present Lord Jesus has the answers to life's most important questions. The all gracious, all loving and all kind Jehovah knows what we are to hunger after. He knows what will fulfill us. He knows what will bring us joy. He knows what will satisfy us beyond anything that this world can create. God in the flesh, Jesus Christ, has a set of activities which He wants us to participate in. Jesus has an ultimate game which He would like us to hunger after as well. It is found when He spoke from a mountain side to a group of followers. They were longing to hear what they should be doing with their lives. He spoke to them then and He speaks to us now. There is indeed something that every man and every woman must hunger after. It is the ultimate hunger game.

In one of our Lord's most famous sermons found in chapter five in Matthew's gospel, Jesus says, "Blessed are those who hunger and thirst for righteousness, for they shall be filled."

There is something which the Lord wants us to hunger for. Though important for many, recognition and acclaim from the world is not what the Lord desires for us to hunger for. Though it may be tempting for ourselves and others, wealth and material possessions are not what the Lord wants us to hunger for. Though knowledge, certifications, degrees and job titles drive

16

many of us daily, our Creator wants something different to captivate our minds and hearts. We often seek after lifeless gods of our own making. He wants us to hunger after His righteousness of His making. This righteousness is the only ambition which will bring enduring happiness and satisfaction.

So what is this righteousness? This righteousness is the desire in one's heart to replace sin with virtue, to replace disobedience with obedience, to replace a hunger to do it our own way with a hunger to serve His will and to do life His way. When we trust in the Lord Jesus as Savior and Lord, He saves us giving us a new heart and eternal life. When we walk with Him moment by moment, He keeps us in His care and purifies us continually. When we hunger for His righteousness, we will be satisfied with a hunger for even more.

I love eating salmon. I can eat it until I cannot eat any more. However, even though my taste and stomach is filled at times, my desire to have a salmon fillet continues to grow and even increases. The very satisfaction which I gain from a great salmon dinner makes me want more. I want to eat more salmon because it is so satisfying. In similar fashion, the person who genuinely hungers for God's righteousness finds it so satisfying that he wants more and more.

What are you starving for? What do you have stomach pains over because you are so hungry for it? This is not a mindset of ho hum. This is a mindset of hunger, intense longing to be filled. Do you have it? I must ask myself the same question. Do I have it? When we do hunger for the Lord's righteousness, we will be filled. Are you a nibbler, wanting only to pick and choose whatever suits your fancy or are you starving for God? If you are hungry, you are ready to receive the Lord's very best.

I will be praying that you seek after His righteousness each and every day. If you do, you will be satisfied.

Scripture reading: Romans 12:1, 2

Draw near to God and He will draw near to you.

Look Before You Reach

As you know by now I really enjoy working in the yard. Though my yard does not come close to being the nicest on the block, I still look forward to getting my hands dirty when yard work calls. It is not only recreation and exercise for me but oftentimes a great sense of satisfaction. It is a sense of accomplishment when something really does comes up from the ground as I planned. Over the years, I feel that I have made some decent decisions concerning my yard plans. However, there have been some decisions which I know that I would do much differently if I had a chance to do it all over again. One of those days crossed my path a few weeks back.

In order to get our flower beds ready for some new fall flowers, I needed to clear the beds of all unwanted debris. In the flower bed just to the right of the front steps there was a large section which needed some clearing. I got most of the large pieces with a rake but some weeds were under a large dogwood and were impossible to get at while standing upright. Casting the rake aside, I got down on my hands and knees and reached deep into the bush pulling and clipping vines as I went. After about 10 minutes of clearing the area just as I wanted it, I stood up and finished the remaining sections on my feet and with the rake in hand. The day ended fairly well with several yard work tasks being accomplished. My work was done for the day but I did not know what I would wake up to the next morning. What I encountered the next morning really threw a damper on the positive memories of yard work that day.

Following my work day in the yard I woke up as normal. However, everything changed when I went into the bathroom passing by our large mirror. I saw and then began to feel red

19

rashes all over my body. I had red pimple like blisters popping up all over my arms, my face, my ears, my stomach and even my legs. As I have since found out, the area where I was clearing had the dreaded three leaf villain. Unknown to me I had been reaching and pulling with bare arms, face, neck, legs and chest into a patch of poison ivy.

Over the next three days, those areas exposed to the poison ivy were a little uncomfortable to say the least. I had a streak of red itchy patches all over my body constantly calling out to be scratched. I felt a little better several days later but only after three different types of ointments had been applied repeatedly.

After thinking about it, I really cannot believe it. I know what poison ivy looks like and I know what it does to me. I have accidently gotten into a patch before and it was awful. When exposed before it had taken a couple weeks for those nasty boils to finally go away. I should have looked through the area first and then been on the lookout for the three leafed menace. In a different setting, a different yard and a different neighborhood I would have been on the lookout. I would not have been comfortable reaching in and around a foreign bush in a different setting. On that Saturday however I was not in a strange place. I was at home. I was in my own yard, in my own environment and in my own territory. As it turned out, I got comfortable and took things for granted. I was totally unaware and totally taken by surprise. I went reaching into a hostile bush not even thinking that anything would harm this old guy. As it turned out, I was dead wrong. I reached in totally confident that I had the yard figured out. So to speak, I had the world in my hands all the while being exposed to beads of skin blistering poison waiting to make my world less than what it should be.

20

Don't let what happened to me, happen to you spiritually. Don't get comfortable in life thinking like I did that Saturday morning. I felt that nothing could harm me. Don't forget that it is a battle out there. It is spiritual warfare each and every day. You need your armor on for if not, like me, your skin will be exposed to a blistering attack of our opponents. Don't reach into settings overconfident. There can be some things laying low which can make your world miserable for a few days or even longer. Don't do what I did and stick your face into a world that oftentimes dishes out some real poison.

As you probably know already, temptation, lust, disobedience and the resulting hurtful sin are always in the bushes just ahead of you. Sometimes it is the quickest and easiest path to just reach in but know this: You reap what you sow. In other words, you always get out of it what you put into it. Better still, if you play with fire you will get burned. If your exposed skin gets poison on it, it will have an adverse affect on your life.

Therefore as the inspired word of the living God says, "Flee youthful lusts." and "Do not be conformed to this world" and "Be as shrewd as snakes and as innocent as doves" "Abstain from sinful lusts which wars against your soul" I Thessalonians 4:7 says "For God did not call us to be impure, but to live a holy life." Finally in James 1:12-15 "Blessed is the man who perseveres under trial, because when he has stood the test, he will receive the crown of life that God has promised to those who love Him."

Hang in there in the battle of life. Be wise in what you decide to put your hands and your face to. Be circumspect and if in doubt call a true friend who can give you some wise counsel. What you do today really does determine who you will become tomorrow. Stay the course with the Lord.

He is your biggest fan pulling for you every step of the way. As always, know that He will never leave you nor forsake you.

Keep working, keep clearing but watch and look before you reach.

Scripture reading: Matthew 10:16

Draw near to God and He will draw to you.

Good Soil

In this area of the country, the last week in September up through the first week in October are grass seeding days. Because it is too hot during the summer months and just too cold for seed to germinate in the winter, most of us who desire to grow grass must wait until the September/October window in the year. It is a fairly simple process but everything must be done exactly right or no grass will come up. There are several essential elements on the way to the creation of a good lawn but traditionally most agree that there are three primary components which must be carefully considered.

The three most common keys to a good lawn include: the quality of the grass seed, the right balance of nitrogen, phosphorus and potassium in the fertilizer and then ample amounts of water. Though these components are extremely important, I would like to add one additional step on the road to growing grass. Before the seed, before the fertilizer and before the water begins to be applied, the soil needs to be prepared. There needs to be a seed bed.

During the first week of October this fall I went to the garage, got out a good pair of work gloves, grabbed my rake and headed to a large patch of yard which was totally bare. After taking a deep breath, I prepared myself for the long and arduous task at hand. I needed to be prepared because the job in front of me was going to need some serious elbow grease. Serious effort was needed because the ground was hard and compacted. I knew what had to take place and so I got after it.

First of all, if the soil was going to be readied, I had to press down one to two inches into the hard soil right out of the gate.

After getting a grip on the soil as best that I could, I would rip towards myself breaking up the compacted soil. Since I had an area about 55 feet long and about 10 feet wide, this first rip was the first of probably 2 to 3 thousand rips. I had my work cut out for me. In only a few minutes, my arms, hands, back and shoulders began to feel the stresses of the work. It was difficult breaking up the hard soil, so hard in fact that I had to take several breaks.

Thinking back on this chore that I finished that morning, I could have chosen to go the easy road. I could have just thrown the grass seed onto the ground, fertilized it and watered it but I knew what the results would have been. The vast majority of the seed would not have taken. It could not have. The seed needed a seed bed. It needed an environment which was receptive and pliable. Then and only then, would the grass grow deep and strong.

Though tough going for nearly two hours and 30 minutes, I finally had a seed bed in which to plant the grass seed. I got out a new bag of grass seed and thoroughly scattered the seed on the readied seed bed. The soil was good. The soil was ready. The soil was prepared to grow what was needed to be grown. All of this came with preparation. All of this came with hard work. All of this came because I knew that the soil needed to be prepared.

While raking the soil that day back in October, I couldn't help but think about my own life. Concerning the Lord and His desire for me to know His will for my life, is my life like this soil? Am I hard and unyielding not able or willing to receive the good seed of the Word, the good seed of His love for me or the good seed of His will for my life? Am I like that red clay? Hard, cracked where parched, and set in my ways? Or, am I a good seed bed,

24

ready and willing to receive what He has for my life? Am I moldable, moveable and able to be used for His good purpose?

As in the gospel of Matthew in chapter 13, I need to ask myself, which type of soil am I when the word of God is sown into my life. "A farmer went out to sow his seed. As he was scattering the seed, some fell along the path, and the birds came and ate it up. Some fell on rocky places, where it did not have much soil. It sprang up quickly, because the soil was shallow. But when the sun came, the plants were scorched, and they withered because they had no root. Other seed fell among thorns, which grew up and choked the plants. Still other seed fell on good soil, where it produced a crop – a hundred, sixty or thirty times what was sown. He who has ears, let him hear."

So I ask you this day, concerning the Lord and His desire to lead you in life, how is the soil of your heart? Are you hard and unyielding wanting to do everything your own way? Is the soil of your mind like concrete so that the pure water of the Word just rolls off, down the street and into the storm drain? Or is your heart and mind, pliable, open, and willing to hear what the Good Lord has to say? Have you humbled yourself under the mighty love of the Lord, ready to hear His call upon your life? Look unto heaven even this very day. Soften your hearts even as you read these words. When you do, your soil is ready and able to receive all the blessings which our Heavenly Father would like to give us. Have a great remainder of the day as you work to soften the soil of your heart and life before the caring and all-wise arms of the Lord.

Scripture reading: Matthew 13:18-23.

Draw near to God and He will draw near to you.

Black Friday and the Deal of a Lifetime

This past Thanksgiving was a wonderful time again this year. We had family in town, ate lots of turkey and got our fill of college and pro football. We sat around the living room and got caught up with family happenings, smiled continuously at the three year old niece and laughed often at University of Michigan jokes. I love the mixture of family, great food and good times.

Over the years, we have done many things for fun at Thanksgiving. We have made a home movie about a human eating golf ball, played touch football in the front lawn and even did bumper car basketball in downtown Chicago. In addition to the renewal of family relationships, there is another Thanksgiving week tradition that is eagerly anticipated every year. It happens on the day after Thanksgiving. It is Black Friday.

As you know, Black Friday is when most every store across the United States opens its doors for deals no man can refuse. Whether it is 75% off or buying three for the price of one, shoppers get to the stores early on Black Friday in search of the deal of a lifetime. The Friday after Thanksgiving this year was no exception. Black Friday was announced and we were right in the thick of it.

At 4:15am Friday morning, the alarm went off in the Floyd household. With my brother-in-law Jim Meeks joining me, we both grabbed a quick slice of pumpkin bread and headed out the door towards our shopping destination. We didn't head for the Mall, nor Belk, nor Kohl's nor JC Penney. No, we headed for every man's shopping destination. We headed for Home Depot. We headed for a sale on tools, equipment and other things that every handyman desperately needs to maintain his abode. At 5am on Black Friday, the Home Depot was going to finally reveal what was sitting under those Black Friday tarps. Jimmy and I were searching for a bargain. We were looking for an offer so good that we could not refuse it. Our quest was for a 'deal of a lifetime'.

Because we got there early, we were able to get to the bargain sections within seconds of the doors opening. Both Jimmy and I grabbed two Werner ladders, two work benches and a cart full of drill bits, lights, work tubs and a compressor. Every item was priced at 60-75% off regular retail. We found some deals which were the best that I had not found for months and possibly all year. Was this year's Black Friday a deal of a lifetime? We found some bargains but I would not say that we found a 'deal of a lifetime'.

Truthfully, in all of my Black Friday excursions over the years, I have found some great prices but none that would fit the category of 'the deal of a lifetime'. For me, in order for something to be considered a 'deal of a lifetime', it would have to be something that I could not find anywhere else. It would have to be so unbelievable that I would never forget it. It would have to be so amazing that I would desire to tell everyone about it. If I found a 'deal of a lifetime' it would really cost me nothing. My only effort would be to just reach out and pick it up. In essence, it would be free.

Black Friday was fun this year and we saved a bunch of money but it was not a 'deal of a lifetime'. Nothing was a free gift. In my life, I have received many gifts, all of which I am extremely grateful. I have received birthday gifts, Christmas morning gifts and accomplishment gifts but I have only had one gift that I would say is a 'deal of a lifetime'. For me, there is only one situation which I would say that the gift was so rare and valuable, that I have never forgotten it. In fact it was such a deal that I have wanted to tell others all about it.

I received the gift that I am talking about in the month of November back in 1980. I received a gift that was the 'deal of a lifetime'. Nothing before and nothing ever after has even come close to the gift I received that day. The day that I accepted Jesus Christ as my Lord and Savior was the 'deal of a lifetime'. In my residence hall room on the campus of Arizona State University in Tempe, Arizona, I received the gift of eternal life. I became a child of God. I received every spiritual blessing available to mankind on that day. I received all of this not by my own effort but only by reaching over and picking it up. I did not have to get up early, fight traffic or pay a price at the cashier. I received it as a gift. It has been the 'deal of a lifetime'.

Holy Scripture tells it best in Ephesians 2:8, 9 "For it is by grace you have been saved, through faith and this not from yourselves, it is the gift of God, not by works, so that no one can boast."

Ephesians 1:3 "Praise be to the God and Father of our Lord Jesus Christ who has blessed us in the heavenly realms with every spiritual blessing in Christ."

John 1:12 "Yet to all who received Him, to those who believe in His name, he gave the right to become children of God."

So I ask you this day, have you found the 'deal of a lifetime'? Have you reached out and received the free gift of eternal life offered to you in the person of Jesus Christ? Have you breathed a prayer that has said something like this: "Dear Lord Jesus, I acknowledge that you died on the cross for my sins and that you rose again on the third day. I believe in you and put my faith and trust in you. I accept you as my savior and my Lord. I know that you are alive and because of my faith in you, I will live forever with you as well. Come into my life and make me into the person that you want me to be. In the name of Jesus, amen."

If you have talked to Jesus and have accepted Him similar to this, you are a believer, a child of God, a follower of Jesus, a Christian. If you have begun this personal relationship with Jesus with a prayer promising to turn from your own selfish ways and towards the Lord's all wise ways, similar to the prayer above, you have received The 'deal of a lifetime'.

Scripture reading: Matthew 7:13-14

Draw near to God and He will draw near to you.

Battle for the Mind

A few evenings back I was able to spend a few minutes on our back deck. I usually get out with the dog each evening and then quickly return indoors but that night I pulled up a chair and relaxed a bit. The interesting thing about that evening was the things which I ignored and the things which I concentrated on. As it turned out, I took no note of the wonderful temperature which surrounded me, nor the beautiful trees which crossed my site line. As I sat in my chair, my physical senses were dormant. However, my mental capacities were alive and well. As I sat in my chair, all I could focus on was not the here and now but the things which happened in my world months ago. Instead of seeing and feeling the current beauty, I was dwelling on my past. Instead of being thankful, I was drifting in thought toward times, events and conversations which were less than my best efforts.

Anyone who knows me well knows that I am capable of making mistakes. When I do make a wrong decision which ends up being painful, most times I forget about it and move on. However, there are some mistakes, especially the ones which have an effect on others, which really takes over my mental focus. When I get off track and forget the Truth that I have learned in the past, I repeatedly find myself being locked into the phrase, "If only." "If only I would have said this. If only I would have held my tongue entirely. If only I would have known. If only I would have been more aggressive. If only I would have been more servant like. If only, if only, if only."

As my mind was taken away on such a useless journey that night, I knew why it was happening. I knew the exact reason why I was letting such corrosive "woe is me" thoughts overtake my thinking. You see, when I do not bath my mind in a certain tub of water, I will reap a specific thought pattern. Nine times out of ten this thought pattern ends up being negative, unforgiving, and vengeful and even plotting to even the score somehow. So that evening when I finally sensed where I was heading mentally, I stopped and got into the tub of water which renews, refocuses, changes, convicts, challenges and encourages all who bath in it. I opened my bible and began to read. The holy bible is that tub of water which I desperately needed.

Turning to the first chapter in Colossians I began to read. I read of Christ's supremacy. I read of His presence in my life. I read about how He wants us to set our minds on Him. I read how we are to let the peace of Christ rule in our hearts. I read of His call for us to let His words dwell in us richly. And finally I read how He wants us to bear one another's burdens, forgive one another, teach one another and challenge one another.

As my eyes began to soak in the pure water of the Word of God, my mind and focus began to change. I forgot about my past foibles and remembered the forgiveness and newness which Christ promises to all who believe. I forgot about the sins and errors committed against me and forgave those individuals remembering how Jesus forgave me. After reading for only a few minutes, I realized once again that the Lord I serve is willing and able to give me the power to overcome and to move on in life past my mistakes, past my failures and past my bad decisions. I read His word and was again reminded of the importance of His viewpoint in my life. I was reminded that His word is the perspective to have. If it is not, then look out, anything and everything can come knocking at the door of your mind.

I know you have lots of things on your minds these days. You have work. You have obligations. You have classes. You have family situations. You have friends and relationship concerns and happenings. You even have thoughts of your future and maybe even thoughts of your past. I know that thoughts come and go as you ponder and pursue your dreams. However, I would like to remind you as I was reminded that evening a few days back, that there is a person who wants to be a part of your thoughts and your dreams. The Lord Jesus Christ is the one who wants in. Through His word, Jesus wants you to look at life through His eyes. He wants you to consider your moves in life through His lenses. He wants you to look at past mistakes, past victories, current disappointments and current victories through His all wise counsel.

So, as you think on your day coming up, look to the Creator, the Master and the Savior. Look to Him when your mind is drifting into muddy waters. Look within the Word of God so you can to bring the real, purposeful, meaningful and Christ-honoring focus back to your life. The lesson that I was reminded of that day was that I need God's Word bathing my mind with its truth each and every day. Therefore, take out the cleansing Word of God and wash in it. If you do, you will move toward having a mind which will see life as it is meant to be seen.

Tomorrow morning, over the lunch hour or maybe even in the evening sometime, take out His word and renew your thoughts. When you do, you will have the ammunition that you need to fight the battle for your mind set before you every day.

Scripture reading: Colossians 3:16

As always, draw near to God and He will draw near to you.

Old Tree in the Middle of the Yard

Though I have been putting off and dreading the day for quite some time, I just couldn't turn a blind eye to it any longer. After over 18 years of it standing tall in the back yard, four children wearing it out with their swings day after day and literally dozens of guests kicking at it, running around it and leaning up against it, the old tree in the middle of the back yard had to be cut down. It had been dead for quite some time and was starting to rot from the inside. It was not safe to leave it up any longer. I called up a friend who runs his own tree service and in less than 10 minutes the good old tree in the middle of our back yard was on the ground.

As you can imagine, watching that big old tree come toppling down was a little emotional for me. That old tree represented a lot of great memories. It was there when we moved into the house. When we moved in, my oldest child was just five years old. She is now 24. That tree has seen many things over the years, from swings to leaves, to hanging posts. I can remember many days when I would push our little ones on those swings. They would be smiling and laughing as they asked me to push them higher and higher.

The old tree in the middle of our back yard would also release a huge crop of leaves each year. Those falling leaves were a calling card for all of my children. When the leaves would start to fall I would yell out "Leaves!" They would then begin to run around the old tree in hopes of catching a leaf before it would hit the ground. If they did get one in flight, I would toss the victor high into the air for each leaf caught.

The old tree served some other purposes as well. Though not so popular with some in my family, the old tree also served as a hanging post for the cleaning of deer. One year we had two deer hanging from the old tree due to the fact that both myself and my youngest son each shot one. The old tree in the back yard also served as the central post for silly string, a hiding spot for air soft war games and a crash pad for a friend of my daughter when the swing carrying her broke one afternoon.

As I started to cut the tree up shortly after my friend laid it on the ground, I was reminded of how time flies. It seemed like only yesterday when that tree had huge branches full of leaves with two blue and yellow swings telescoping down from each side. Time truly marches on at a steady pace. As I can attest, time moves so steadily and quickly that before you know it you are cutting down a tree which used to be a center of activity. Though I know it all too well, our tendency is to hurry through those times anxiously awaiting the next task on the list. Oftentimes we blow through life never really stopping to make the most of the situations and opportunities set before us.

The good Lord talks about the brevity of life often in His Word. Ephesians 5:16 says, "…making the most of the time…Psalm 90:12 says "teach us to number our days that we might gain a heart of wisdom."

What are you doing these days to make the most of the time given to you? Are you doing and being the person that the Good Lord would have you do and be? Are you taking time to commune with your Maker? Are you taking time to read and/or discuss with others what He has to say about life in His

34

Word? Are you truly encouraging and making those around you better? Are you giving your absolute best in whatever you are choosing to put your hands to? Are you modeling a faith-filled life before a watching world? As you know they are looking for answers to life's most important questions. If you are doing all of these things with your time, then keep it up. The Lord wants us to rest in Him, reload in Him and enjoy Him. In His presence truly is fullness of joy.

Even though it is difficult to think about, all of us are like that tree in the middle of the back yard. All of us will have a time when we are growing, bearing leaves and standing strong in the storms of life. All of us will enjoy a time when we are the center of attention with possibly many individuals enjoying our shade, our limbs and our leaves. Then there will be a time when we will become old. Like the old tree, we too will eventually cast off this tree trunk of life on this earth. When that time comes, may those who have surrounded our lives have volumes and volumes of memories of our making a difference in their life. Before the Good Lord takes us home, giving permission for our tree to come down, may all of us have such an impact on the lives of others that they will never forget our love, our faith, our service and our life.

Have a great day. Keep the faith. Live the faith and share the faith through your lives and words. Continue to grow strong and bear many leaves. Cast your shade upon many this coming week and may others enjoy your presence in their lives just as we thoroughly enjoyed the old tree in the middle of the yard.

Scripture reading: I Corinthians 10:31

Draw near to God and He will draw near to you.

The Perfect Gift

If you were not done with your Christmas shopping by Christmas Eve, you probably were in some trouble. As I know all too well, waiting until Christmas Eve to find that perfect present makes shopping like a NFL playoff game. It is very competitive and difficult to win. Unless you had good protection from mad approaching lineman and were able to spot some open receivers, you may have had a tough time. Usually the selection options are dwindling fast by Christmas Eve. If you were a computer guy and confident that you could make your last minute purchases by just pointing and clicking away, that plan was probably in jeopardy as well. As you know, on-line ordering may not have been able to guarantee an overnight delivery for Christmas morning. Finally, if you were a brave soul and were willing to attack the mall, I am sure that it was an experience. The traffic was probably crazy and more than likely the lines at every check-out stand were long. Nevertheless, if you were like the rest of us, you did whatever it took to find that perfect present for those loved ones in your life. You will face the crowds, bump shoulder to shoulder with grandmas and do what it takes to find that gift which is just right for those on your list.

Finding the perfect present is the goal especially if it is for those close to you in life. If you have a little brother, you will hunt until you get what he would like. If you have a younger or older sister, you will find out what she likes and then shop until you find something as close to her desires as possible. And then for the parents, though they claim to have everything, you will put some time into it and think of something special for them. For all of those in your life who you love, you will do what you can to put something under the tree just for them. Christmas time is a wonderful time that we all can visibly show that we truly care for all of those close to our hearts.

The perfect gift is the goal but it can be very elusive as well. It is a moving target because we cannot read our recipients mind or heart. We cannot know for sure what they would like. We cannot know for sure what they really need. We can notice the things on the outside but we can never see the inside stuff. For example, we can notice that they do not have a good pair of shoes, a jacket to stay warm or a phone, but we can never notice what they need on the inside of their hearts. We can observe what is missing on the outside but we are only guessing as to what they need on the inside. The inside of life is not really our realm to address anyway. Gifts that address the inside is an area that is really reserved for another who is more qualified to address such things.

This gift giver that I am talking about is the One who knows exactly what we need. He not only knows what we would like to have, he also knows what we dislike, what we fear, what we are anxious about, what we take courage in as well as what we dread. This perfect gift giver is able to see beyond what we may show on the outside and goes much deeper to who we really are on the inside. This perfect gift giver knows us completely and is standing by with an armful of gifts meant to meet our needs completely. This perfect gift giver has proven Himself years ago by fighting the crowds, fighting the insults, fighting the scourging, fighting the cross and fighting death being victorious in all such challenges in order to deliver the perfect gift to us. This perfect gift giver always delivers on time and always delivers what He says that He will deliver. He always gives whether we are living in plenty or in want. He always gives beyond all that what we could ever ask or imagine.

This perfect gift giver knows us better than we know ourselves and gives us exactly what we need at the time. He is there for us and will never leave us nor ever forsake us.

As you probably know, this perfect gift giver is the master of all, the Lord Jesus Christ. He is the One who gives gifts that no store, no person or no job could deliver. He gives perfectly meeting our deepest most important needs for every man or woman. He gives gifts that will not only never wear out, but they will last a lifetime. More than that, they will last for all of eternity. This perfect gift giver, when individuals accept Him as their Lord and Savior, then He will totally unload His armful of gifts to all who believe. Every spiritual blessing in the heavenlies will be bestowed upon all who will just believe and follow. When we believe on Him, some of His perfect gifts will be as follows: He gives us perfect cleansing from our sins. He gives us His perfect presence. He gives us His perfect peace. He gives us His perfect power. He gives us His perfect purpose; purpose that will impact a world scrambling to find gifts that will only fade away. He gives eternal life.

"He who believes in the Son has everlasting life." John 3:36

"For God so loved the world that He gave His only begotten Son that whosoever believes in Him shall have not perish but shall have eternal life." John 3:16

"For by grace you have been saved through faith, and that not of yourselves, it is the gift of God." Ephesians 2:8

On Christmas day, when you were thinking about those perfect gifts for your loved ones, know that there is another gift that is THE perfect gift. It will deal with the inside. Know that God came in the flesh, was born in a stable, lived a sinless life, performed miracles before men, went to the cross and was resurrected on the third day. Know that Jesus Christ is the gift that can address the needs of the inside. Believe on Him this day and you will have eternal life. Share it with another and they too will begin the life that we all are meant to live.

As you continue the hunt for those gifts on those special days yet to come, know that the perfect gift has already been bought and paid for. This perfect gift came in the person of Jesus Christ and He is available to every person, on every continent, for all time.

Merry Christmas, once again. May we all be reminded of the greatest and most perfect gift ever given to mankind. May we all live it every day and give it away as He gave Himself to us.

Scripture reading: Romans 6:23

Draw near to God and He will draw near to you.

An Oil Change

I finally got a few minutes the other day to get something done which needed to be done for the last month or so. I finally got the chance to change the oil in the truck. After realizing that I had not changed the oil for the past 5,000 miles, I took the opportunity on a Sunday afternoon and got it done. Since I like to change the oil in our cars myself, I stopped by NAPA Autoparts and got five quarts of 5W-30. I already had a filter so I was set.

First of all, I got out a large oil pan in order to catch the oil. Then I proceeded to crawl under the truck. I had a socket set that fit the screw on the oil case under the engine so I removed the nut and proceeded to empty the truck of its old black oil. When it came out, I was glad that I did not wait any longer to change it. It was thin and black. As you know, oil that is thin and black is not the kind of oil that will keep an old truck engine running.

After draining the oil, I then reached up alongside the V6 engine and found the filter. Since it was just tightened by hand, I easily loosened the filter and removed it. When I put the new filter on, I filled the engine with five and a half quarts of new NAPA oil. My truck was finally back to where it needed to be. With new oil and a new filter in place, I am now confident that the truck engine will have the right lubricants in which to perform appropriately.

With the changed oil, I believe my truck is now set for another 5,000 miles. We are good to go for another four to five months but I do realize that it is not forever. We are good to go for now but only until the oil has turned black and thin again. We are good to go for today but only until the filter stops screening the particles which harms car engines. We are good to go for a while but only for just that, for a while. When the mileage and engine time comes up again, we will have to do it all over again. It felt good to change the oil on that Sunday but it also reminded me that very soon it will be time to change it again. Changing the oil was important and it needed to be done, but it also was a reminder to me that my fix is not permanent. Changing the oil will not give me a new engine. It may possibly prolong the life of my truck's engine but it will not make it new.

There are lots of things in life which only serve to remind us that we must do certain things again eventually. We may eat breakfast this morning but soon afterward we know that we will need to eat again. We may workout, but we will have to workout again if we are going to move toward our fitness goals. We may save a hundred dollars this paycheck but we must do it again and again if we want to get even close to our savings goals. In most every sphere of life whether it be relationship building, educational growth or fitness goals, our efforts are never a one and done. We may choose to be kind to a friend only to be reminded that we must constantly be investing in the relationship in order for it to grow. Every area of life seems to be like that. However, there is one area in life where there is an exception to this rule.

There is an area in life where something once done is done and settled forever. It is not an oil change that will soon be needed to be changed again. It is something that is forever. There is something in life which is like a permanent oil change.

"I really want to stop but I just can't help it." "I really want to not think like that but I just seem to return there mentally every time." "I really want to change but I just don't think that I can." All of these statements have come from individuals who have been going through life receiving only 5,000 mile oil changes.

None of them seem to help however. Why? Because they are still the same person. They have never received the gift of life which is forever. They have never received the permanent oil change.

II Corinthians 5:17 says "Therefore if any man be in Christ he is a new creation. Old things have passed away and behold all things have become new."

If you do not want your life to be on a human effort management plan, if you want your life to be changed from the inside out, if you want your life to be new and changed forever, such a picture is possible. It is not a dream. It is not wishful thinking. It is within our reach. It is within your reach. You do not have to be an oil change knowing that you will just have to do it all over again in a few months. No, you can be a new creation. You can have a new heart. You can have a new start, a new beginning. Listen to the author of these promises once again:

John 10:10 Jesus speaking, "I have come that they may have life and have it more abundantly."

I John 5:12 "He who has the Son has life; he who does not have the Son does not have life."

John 1:12 "Yet to all who received Him, to those who believe in His name, He gave the right to become children of God."

John 10:28 Jesus speaking, "I give them eternal life, and they shall never perish; no one can snatch them out of my hand."

I John 5:13, "I write these things to you who believe in the name of the Son of God so that you may know that you have eternal life."

And Isaiah 1:18 "Come let us reason together" says the Lord. "Though your sins are like scarlet, they shall be white as snow; though they are red as crimson, they shall be like wool."

If we believe in Him, if we trust in Him, if we accept Him as the Lord and Savior of our lives, we too can walk in newness of life. We too can have a permanent oil change never having to change it again. Will we sin? Yes. Will we need to confess our sins to the Lord? Yes. But, we will always be His son, in His family, never able to be plucked from His hand, watched over, cared for, and indwelt with His presence.

If you have never trusted in the Lord Jesus Christ, accept Him into your life even this day. If you do, I promise you, the Lord promises you, that it will be the best decision that you will ever make.

It will make a difference in this life and your eternal life to come.

Scripture reading: Matthew 4:19-20

Draw near to God and He will draw near to you.

Friendships Over the Years

Who would drive seven hours, stay at the location for eight hours only to drive back seven hours all in the same day? Who would stop by four different locations, skip lunch, be constantly entering new addresses in the Garmin and finally get dinner around 8pm? Why would anyone want to get up at 4:20 in the morning and return at 3:30am? Who would travel such a distance and return so late only to say that they would do it all over again in a heartbeat?

The only answer to such a weekend schedule is that there must have been something at the other end of this journey that was so attractive, so enjoyable and so rewarding that the tiredness, the soreness and the time on the road was a welcome price to pay.

This past Saturday Debbie and I drove to Columbus, Ohio and back in one day. We made the trip primarily to be a part of the 25th wedding anniversary of a wonderful couple whose wedding my wife was a part of many years ago. Since our 25th was last summer, our intent was to only go to the anniversary celebration but we found ourselves doing much more. We found ourselves crossing the paths of several others who made the trip even more special than it already was.

In addition to seeing Stephanie and Robert's celebration, we spoke to old friends which included Trent, Matt and Sue, and Dan and Debbie. It was wonderful and we would do it again at the drop of a hat.

The trip was so rich because of the people we saw. When our eyes met and our voices connected for some of us it had been over 15 years since we had last seen each other. However, though the years had separated us, within minutes we were speaking freely to one another just like we had done on a regular basis years before. It was wonderful to hear what the Lord was doing in their lives, how family were getting along and what things lay on the horizon. Just like years before, we were encouraged, were challenged and were extremely joyful and sad when we finally said our goodbyes.

How does that happen? How is it possible that friendships which were formed years earlier still be so full? How is it that only after a few minutes of conversation that you feel like you had been in touch with them throughout the entire time of separation? I believe this happens because of the relationship that was forged between us years before. Our friendship continues because at one time we: needed each other, listened to each other, did things together, laughed together, shared together, cried together, stepped out in faith together, trusted the Lord together, opened up God's Word together, had meals together, shared life goals together, suffered life's disappointments and trials together, and experienced life's joys and blessings together.

You see we did life together. We were shoulder to shoulder when we needed friends who, like us, were striving to look at life through the same life lenses. These dear friends had put on the same lenses of a personal relationship with the Lord Jesus Christ and they were right where we were. In their presence was affirmation. In their presence was encouragement. In their presence was understanding. In their presence was a desire to be and do all that the Lord would have us be and do. We were young husbands, young wives, young moms, and young dads breaking trail on the path of life.

Though the passage of time may once again creep in, I am confident that these friends will be friends forever. Deep friendships which are bound together happen when you have something very important in common. Since accepting Jesus as savior is so important and special, there is a potential for a wonderful relationship with another who have done the same. Having a relationship with another who loves the Lord and is striving to live for Him can span time and distance. Such friendships are available but you must do a little hunting for them. Such friendships are out there waiting for us to enjoy but we must grow one big friendship before you can grow all others.

In order to become the kind of friend that we all need in our lives, we must first start by knowing the greatest friend that you can ever have. In order to have an impact like these true friends have had with us, we much start with the Lord Jesus Christ and get to know Him. In order to be a friend who is a friend forever, we must do a few things which the author of friendship recommends. A few things in this friendship with the Lord may include: that we read what Jesus says, see what He does, feel for others how he feels, model how He lives, think with His mind and walk with Him moment by moment.

Once this friendship with Jesus is solid and ongoing, we can be the kind of friend who makes a difference in another's life. After we have begun this walk with Jesus, then we can start looking for those individuals within our reach who we may drive miles to see some day. We can then start looking for those on which we can practice the 'One Another's' highlighted in Holy Scripture. Some of these include: Start loving one another - I John 4:7, 8. Begin praying for one another - James 5:16, Bear with each other and forgive whatever grievances you may have against one another - Colossians 3:13, serve one another in love- Galatians 5:13, and Encourage one another-Hebrews 10:25.

In time, as you walk with your Lord and practice these 'One Another's', you will have opportunities to build your relationship with the Lord as well as with those individuals who are in your life.

Then someday, I hope and pray that you too will say to yourself, "I would drive seven hours to see these dear friends all over again.

Scriptures: Proverbs 18:24

Draw near to God and He will draw near to you.

Inside Out,

New Year's Resolutions

January 5th was an interesting day this year. It was day number five into the New Year. How were you doing at that point? On January 5th how were you doing with all of those pledges that you said to yourself and possibly others just a few days earlier? Specifically, how were all of your New Year's resolutions coming? Yes, January 5th was early in the process so maybe I should check back later. Maybe I should check back in a week, a month or maybe even in six months. I can then ask how you are doing.

Making resolutions to make a change is common to most of us. It is common because we all have things in our lives that we would like to address. We all have things that we would like to start doing. We also have things that we would like to stop doing. The choice of what goes onto our New Year's resolution list may come from a variety of sources. One item on the ledger may come from our bathroom scale. Another may come from a physician examining our medical report. It may come from a collection agency inquiring about an unpaid bill. It may come from a supervisor at our year end review. It may come from an old friend who has noticed the way that you have handling family relationships. It may come from a pastor talking about God's will for our lives. There are all kinds of sources for the things that go on our New Year's resolution list.

However, most topics that end up on resolution lists do not come from an outside source. They come from our own heart and mind. A good New Year's resolution comes from the honest evaluation of our current state of affairs. They come to us as we ponder our performance in the key dimensions of life. Such dimensions may include: academic endeavors, health and fitness, finances, relationships, community and the spiritual.

We know that making resolutions can help to give us focus but why are they so difficult to keep? Why is it so common that most are broken in a very short time? Why is it that while we start out sincere and seemingly committed that we end up letting it slip away when the slightest obstacle crosses our path?

There are a few ideas on the why most do not follow through on their New Year's resolutions. Behaviorists would say that some are just not ready to change. They do not have the right amount of will power. Others would say that we are not educated enough on the behavior desired. They say that we are ignorant of the triggers that trip us up. Still other experts would claim that we do not have the right accountability partners in our lives. In other words, we do not have the team assembled to help us accomplish the behavior desired. Lack of will power, lack of knowledge and lack of an accountability partner may help but they will only take us so far.

If you are anything like me I want change that is forever. I can never get it from a to-do list or a prohibition. Change that is forever is always from the inside out. Stating a behavior to acquire or a habit to stop is not where we should begin. Attitudes and behaviors are only outward signs or results of an inward perspective. They are but a result of life view. The problem with most life views is that most do not have the power to do what we are looking for. "Do this", "Don't do that" etc does not change the heart. There is only one thing that can change your heart and thus your life view thereby giving you the needed power to change. It is not a plan, not a list, not a prohibition.

Change that is forever is the result of knowing a person, yielding to a person, having this person work in you and through you. Change is responding to the invitation to be lead by this person and guided by this person. Change is choosing to allow this person to live and work through you. Change that lasts more than a month can occur if we choose to be led by, walk in, and filled by this person. Only then can our lives be truly changed from the inside out. Who is this person? This is person is the one who was fully man and fully God, Jesus Christ. Who gives us the power to do make change real? He is the Holy Spirit.

John 15:4, 5 says Jesus speaking, "Abide in Me, and I in you. As the branch cannot bear fruit of itself, unless it abides in the vine, neither can you, unless you abide in Me." "I am the vine, you are the branches. He who abides in Me, and I in him, bears much fruit, for without Me you can do nothing."

Philippians 4:13 "I can do all things through Christ who strengthens me."

Change is through Jesus Christ.

As you ponder the New Year set before you, I urge you to allow Jesus Christ, through the power of the Holy Spirit to help you achieve the goals that He has laid on your heart. As Colossians 2:21-23 reminds us, man-made regulations only go so far.

"…why as though living in the world, do you subject yourselves to regulations – "Do not touch, do not taste, do not handle." Which all concern things which perish with the using – according to the commandments and doctrines of men? These things indeed have an appearance of wisdom in self-imposed religion, false humility, and neglect of the body, but are of no value against the indulgence of the flesh."

Thanks for your partnership in this great calling. Thanks for all that you do as you shine like stars in a world desperately in need of a savior who can change each and every one of them from the inside out, permanently and forever. Thanks be to God.

Scripture reading: Galatians 6:15

Draw near to God and He will draw near to you.

Moving Water or Frozen Pipes

It was a cold night a few days back. The temperature got down to around zero. When I finally got to my desk the following morning, it still was only six degrees. That blast of cold air took us all by surprise and pushed most of us indoors if we had a choice. We were doing just fine last week and then bam, an Alberta clipper dipped way down into the south ruffling all of our routines. Instead of leisurely walks, people made fires in fireplaces. Instead of working outside, folks were wrapped up in blankets reading books. Instead of short sleeved shirts being worn, large goose down Eddie Bauer jackets came out of closets all across our city. What was normally a fairly mild climate became harsh this past week. Shivers, quivering lips and people jumping up and down while standing were commonplace.

On days like the other day you really understand why people choose to live in the Sunbelt. On days when it is six degrees outside, you can totally understand why individuals move to Southern California, Arizona and Florida. In those places there are no sudden blasts of cold air. In those places the temperature is consistent day in and day out.

Because it was going to be in the single digits the other night, I had to do some things around the house to insure that we would avoid a disaster the following morning.

Since the temperature was so low, there was a good chance that our pipes would freeze. If pipes freeze, the expansion of the water would more than likely burst the pipes allowing gallons of water to come into the house. As I have experienced before, such a happening would necessitate the replacement of sections of

52

pipe, ceiling repair and stoppage of activity in that area for quite some time.

However, there are a few ways to avoid such an event in a home when cold snaps do pass through. The first is to increase the temperature inside the home. The second is to open all of the cabinets beneath piping areas especially underneath sinks. The third and most important method to prevent the freezing of pipes is to keep a stream of water coming out of a faucet throughout the entire day and evening until the cold snap is over. When you keep the water moving through the pipes, it never has a chance to freeze. Because it is always moving forward through the pipes, there is never a time when it is stagnant, stationary and vulnerable to freezing in place. We performed all of these things and our pipes did not freeze. We avoided damage, the loss of home usage in that area and of course the cost of a repair.

So I ask you this day, in your spiritual life, are you keeping the water moving through your pipes? Or, are you frozen spiritually? Are you doing what you need to do in order to avoid stagnation? Or, is the water stopped and vulnerable to a deep freeze? Are you checking the temperature outside and getting prepared when the conditions will be challenging? If not, you really need to get the water moving.

In order to keep your home spiritually safe, you need to start the water back flowing as well. One way is by continually speaking to the Lord through prayer. Another way is to repeatedly open up His word of life and drink of its wisdom, its encouragement and its hope. Finally, you need to meet with other believers desiring to keep the water moving through their pipes as well.

You need to follow the necessary disciplines of the Christian life and raise the temperature in the home, open the cabinets in our lives for inspection and then, most importantly, we need to turn on the faucet. We need to turn on the faucet of our Lord's presence each and every moment of each and every day. When we do such things, our pipes will never freeze. When we do such things on a consistent basis, our spiritual homes will be open for usage every day, potential setbacks and damage can be limited and we will be who our Lord would have us to be.

Hebrews 3:3b-4, 6 "... inasmuch as He who built the house has more honor than the house. For every house is built by someone, but He who built all things is God." vs. 6 "but Christ as a Son over His own house, whose house we are if we hold fast the confidence and the rejoicing of the hope firm to the end."

And according to I Peter 2:4-5 "Coming to Him as to a living stone, rejected indeed by men, but chosen by God and precious, you also, as living stones, are being built up a spiritual house, a holy priesthood, to offer up spiritual sacrifices acceptable to God through Jesus Christ."

If we are going to be that house built by God, that spiritual house, we need to never freeze up. We need to keep the water of the Lord God Almighty moving in our lives. When we allow this to happen, we will be and do everything that our loving Heavenly Father would want us to be and do.

As you enter this coming week and worship on Sunday, may we all know the conditions outside and keep the spiritual water moving.

See you at the faucet.

Scripture reading: Psalms 1:1-3

Draw near to God and He will draw near to you.

Power Lines that Never Go Down

One evening this past winter, lots of people were without power. Some reporters said that close to 500,000 homes were off line. Individuals in these homes had no heat and no hot water. There were no power outlets for refrigerators, freezers, microwaves, ovens, computers or televisions. In some areas, stoplights were not working, schools were closed and businesses were anxiously waiting to open. Everything was shut down and people were not able to do what they would like to do. Everything was cut off and people were not able to go about their lives in a normal way. There was no power for them.

Winter storm "Pax" was the culprit blanketing the southeast dropping loads of snow and freezing rain on roadways, roof tops and tree canopies. The impact was expansive. Some broadcasters have said that the reach of this storm was historical. Beginning in Texas and continuing up through Louisiana, Georgia and the Carolinas, this storm dumped as much as 18 inches in some areas. Transformers, power lines and substations were not supplying power to literally thousands and thousands of people. People had no power.

Without access to power the type of life that we experience is less than it can be. Without power, we actually go back in time eliminating progress that we have enjoyed for years. Without power, we use candlesticks instead of light bulbs, fireplaces instead of electric heat pumps and ink pens instead of Microsoft word. Without power, it seems like the immense expanse and speed of human potential is curtailed to a snail's pace. Without power, we cannot do what we are capable of doing. Life is less than it should be because many are without power.

How about you this day? Are you without power? Have you lost access to the main grid? Have you been limited in what you would like to do because you have no power? Do you have access to energy, to food and to the potential to be and do everything that you would like to be and do this day? Your answer may be "Yes, our home has not lost power. I am fine." But that is not the power source that I am talking about. I am talking about another power source. I am talking about the ultimate power source which gives true energy, true food, true comfort and true experience to life. I am talking about being connected to the One who supplies all of this on a moment by moment, day by day basis. I am talking about the ultimate One who never blows a transformer, never has lines down, never is unavailable to all who desire to have what only He can provide.

Psalm 62:11 "That power belongs to God."

Psalm 68:35 "…is He who gives strength and power to His people."

Matthew 6:13 "For Yours is the kingdom and the power and the glory forever."

Romans 1:16 "For I am not ashamed of the gospel of Christ, for it is the power of God to salvation for everyone who believes…" and Ephesians 1:17-19 "…that the God of our Lord Jesus Christ, the Father of glory, may give to you the spirit of wisdom and revelation in the knowledge of Him, that the eyes of your understanding being enlightened, that you may know what is the hope of His calling, what are the riches of the glory of His inheritance in the saints, and what is the exceeding greatness of His power toward us who believe, according to the working of His great power…"

Are you truly connected this day? Are you one of the hundreds of thousands of people who were without power during winter storm Pax? Or, are you one of the many who moment by moment, day by day are connected to the Lord God Almighty? He is One who has an endless supply of power to all who will believe and follow.

Situations can be tough. Life can be difficult. However, at our disposal is the One who created life, who created the universe, who created you. If He is such an awesome God who is able and willing to give you the power that you need in whatever your circumstance, wouldn't you want to be connected? Wouldn't you want to have access to what He gives to all who will seek His mind, seek His heart, seek His perspective day by day? You can receive the power. You can receive the ability to overcome but you must be connected. You will receive the needed spiritual food, spiritual wisdom, meaning, purpose and joy but you need to get plugged in.

So I ask you, have you at one time, acknowledged that you have gone your own way, were separated from God because of your sin but then subsequently accepted His forgiveness by personally accepting the Jesus Christ as your Lord and Savior of your life? In essence, have you acknowledged His life and death on the cross for your sins believing that He rose again for you?

If you have, then you are connected. You have every spiritual blessing available to you. However, even though you have trusted in Him at one time, are you walking with Him now? There is a possibility that you may be connected but the wire has been frayed. Have you confessed any known sin in your life? Many times we wonder why He is not showing power in our lives when the problem may be that it is us. The issue may be that we are grieving and quenching the Holy Spirit who is this power who is at work in our lives. We do not keep in step because we are holding and not confessing our sins to the Lord. However, once we do, He is then free again to continue His work in our lives which He promises that He will do if we let Him.

When the power was restored to the southeast a few days later, hundreds of thousands will still remain without spiritual power. Was that you? Or, will you join the many others who have found the ultimate power source of life? The power is not a substation. It is not a power line. The ultimate power source is a person and His name is Jesus. Plug in today and stay plugged in day by day for only then will you see life and live life as our Creator would have it lived.

Enjoy the snow when it comes. Also, enjoy the warmth and countless privileges of having power. It has been the best decision that I have ever made in life.

I hope and pray that we will all know and experience it day by day no matter what the weather is outside. Have a great day.

Scripture reading: Philippians 4:13

Draw near to God and He will draw near to you.

Every Waking Second

During the first two weeks of the month of December this year, I honestly have to admit that my mind was elsewhere. When at work it was in a certain location. When at home it was in the same place as well. Even when I was at my son's events, listening to a lecture and on car rides between venues, my mind repeatedly drifted to the same exact destination. How can things like this so consume us in our thoughts? How can we be where we are physically but mentally we really are a million miles away? How can our minds be so focused that every waking second you are planning a pathway to get back to where you were only moments before?

Have you ever been where I have been over the past couple weeks? Have you ever been so engaged in a topic, in an event, in a person, in a game or in a task on the to-do list that every waking second is centered around the next opportunity to get back after it? That was my story this past December. No, I was not caught up in a vice which can seriously wound us from the inside out. No, I was not caught up in an activity which can take away the numerous joys of life. I was caught up in something that needed to be done. I was enthralled in an activity which on the outside was totally acceptable but on the inside was providing a continual lens through which I viewed my day. This item of focus never ended. One thing always leads to another and before long every free minute was caught up with the item which had my thoughts and my attention. The thing which had taken my mind was putting lights around my front yard for Christmas.

For those of you who have been at my house over the holidays, you may have noticed that we have a pretty good amount of green space. I have a front yard, a side lot and a good sized back yard. This past Christmas I wanted to cover the entire perimeter with lights. For those who have such square footage themselves, getting a yard ready with decorations takes some time. Every year during the first two weeks of December this call of the yard begins its incessant howl. Each morning, lunchtime and evening the cries for my attention come calling. At this time of the year, decorating the front yard takes over my mind and the desire to keep putting out more lights never seems to let go. It is over now, but was a real eye opener to see how thoroughly my priorities can shift to a list that was not even on the radar just a month earlier.

So I ask myself and you all this day, what can I learn from this? What can I glean from my focus being so consumed over those weeks in December? How can I allow such a neutral thing like putting lights out to grow into such a level of focus? What life lesson can I take away from the time spent out in the cold desiring to lay lights every day? As in the case with most of life's experiences which come our way, the only way to understand what is out in front of us and oftentimes what is overtaking us is to look up. We need to look to the creator of the mind, the creator of work, the creator of our opportunities and ask for His view on our day to day world.

You see the Lord God Almighty wants our hearts and our minds as the yard had my mind those weeks in December. Jesus Christ wants us to keep Him in such high importance in our thoughts and lives that no matter where we are, no matter what we are doing and no matter where we are going, our thoughts and minds are on His will, His grace, His mercy, His love and His presence in our lives. The Lord God desires for us to be so focused on our relationship with Him that we see Him in all that we put our hands to. Evidence of a focus on Him will bear fruit in our lives as we live for Him moment by moment, day by day and week by week. As the decorations drew enjoyment in my life, the work which the Lord has for us will always be for our ultimate good and enjoyment as well. In His presence is fullness of joy. With a continual focus on Him and His work in our life, we will rest in a life which will be full of purpose, full of power and full of peace. When we think on the Lord as I was thinking of laying lights, we will grow to know Him and love Him just as we have been created to do. And, it all starts with our minds.

In Romans 12:1, 2 God's word says "I urge you therefore my brethren, by the mercies of God to present your bodies a living sacrifice holy and acceptable to God, which is your reasonable service. And do not be conformed to this world but be transformed by the renewing of your mind that you may prove what is good and acceptable and perfect will of God."

Ephesians 4:20-24, "But you have not so learned Christ, if indeed you have heard Him and have been taught by Him, as the truth is in Jesus: that you put off, concerning your former conduct, the old man which grows corrupt according to deceitful lusts, and be renewed in the spirit of your mind, and that you put on the new man which was created according to God, in true righteousness and holiness."

Colossians 3:1-5 "If then you were raised with Christ, seek those things which are above, where Christ is, sitting at the right hand of God. Set your mind on things above, not on things on the earth. For you died, and your life is hidden with Christ in God. When Christ who is our life appears, then you also will appear with Him in glory. Therefore, put to death your members which are on the earth: fornication, uncleanness, passion, evil desire, and covetousness, which is idolatry."

II Corinthians 10:5 "For the weapons of our warfare are not carnal but mighty in God for pulling down strongholds, casting down arguments and every high thing that exalts itself against the knowledge of God, bringing everything thought into captivity to the obedience of Christ."

Be consumed in life, but be consumed on the right things. Be caught up in life but be caught up with our Maker. Go ahead and drift off in thought but drift off in the direction of the One who knows you better than you know yourself. He loves you and is so concerned about your well-being that He died for you. So this coming week, find space in your thoughts for your Lord. Find space as you drive in to work, as you walk to classes, as you sit down for a meeting, as you do yard work. Think on things above, where our Lord is.

When you do, you will be pleasing the Lord our God and drawing close to Him. He truly calls us to love Him will all of our heart, all of our soul, all of our minds and all of our strength.

Scripture reading: Proverbs 23:7

Draw near to God He will draw near to you.

The Fog

It was an eerie yet beautiful view the other evening coming home from work. Fog was everywhere. It was not only apparent in the low lying areas where it is typically located but it was also on the elevated ridges and hills. As I continued my drive home, my mind drifted back to a time many years ago on a river in Ohio. The fog the other night reminded me of a canoe trip which I took with some good friends of mine. It was a trip in the fog.

The trip started out well and then like my drive home a thick blanket of fog roll in covering all that was in front of us. As we paddled down the river, our vision eventually got to where we could only see the tip of the canoe and to either side where the oars were cutting the water. When we started out on the much anticipated river pursuit, we could see everything. We could see the banks, the rocky bottom, the low hanging branches and the turns awaiting us. I can remember how excited and confident we were as we embarked upon a journey much anticipated. All of that turned south when the fog rolled in. Instead of seeing everything in front of us, all we could see was the front of the boat.

After several minutes of paddling blindly, we finally came to the conclusion that we were not going to be able to use our eyes to navigate. Since one of the guys in the other boat had been on the river before and another guy in our boat had seen the map before we put into the river we forged ahead. Instead of stopping or turning around, we continued to paddle forward really not knowing what was ahead. We trusted the guys who had been on the river before, did our best to recall the map and just paddled on. Then in a moment that I have never forgotten, a thought came to my mind. I said it out loud to both of the boats.

I said, "Guys, isn't this like our walks with Christ at times? Many times aren't we in a boat surrounded by fog and we cannot see where we are going? Isn't it true that at times in our lives we only see what is at the end of the boat yet we paddle on? Isn't our trust in the Lord much like what we have in front of us today? We walk by faith and not by sight." One of the guys turned to me and said "That is true Max. We do walk by faith and not by sight."

So this day as you are paddling forward in life, working at your desk, hanging out with friends, starting a required project or watching the game on Fox, what are your sight lines? Can you see very far down the path of life? If you are anything like me, the answer is no. We cannot see the path oftentimes. We cannot see and guarantee a safe uneventful passage. We do not know what is just under the surface. We don't know if there will be waterfalls or debris just around the corner. No, what we do is to just keep putting the oars into the water one after the other and live by faith. We trust in the Lord with all of our hearts and we lean not on our own understanding. We put our faith in the One who knows all, the one who knows the river, knows the boat, knows the oars and knows the companions who will accompany us.

As you embark on another day, as you set your schedule, as you make your plans, do so with this thought in mind. As II Corinthians 5:7 says, "Walk by faith and not by sight." Do your best to see through the fog but also know that none of us know for sure what is ahead. None of us know what kind of victory, what kind of challenge, what kind of heartache and what kind of blessing awaits us. Nevertheless, also know this, The Lord is in control. He knows you and loves you more than you can ever imagine. He cares for you and has plans which are ultimately for your good. Rocks might hit your boat. Low hanging limbs may even hit you upside the head from time to time. Nevertheless, know that all things happen together for the good for those who love God and are called according to His purpose.

I would love for you all to have a clear view of the river in front of you with no obstacles ever to get in your way. However, the good Lord wants us to trust Him regardless of the journey's ride. Trust Him and know that He will never leave you nor forsake you no matter how rough or how smooth the rowing is. So I ask you this day: Are you trusting Him? Are you walking by faith believing God that He will direct your paths? Or, are you worrying, controlling and always depending on what your eyes can see? Yes, paddle hard, pursue excellence and work as hard as you can but know this: fog is normal. Fog is good. Fog helps us to turn our mind and faith to Him. Walk by faith and not by sight.

Scripture reading: Hebrews 11:6

Draw near to God and He will draw near to you.

Irrigation Plans

Southern California finally got a full day of rain yesterday. They have been nearly 11 inches under normal so they were desperate for some movement from the skies. Though I am sure that many activities had to move indoors all across that beautiful state, I am thankful for what the heavens released yesterday. It was not a gully washer with most of its contents shooting into storm drains. No, supposedly it was a steady, soaking rain which gave the parched vegetation the opportunity to slowly absorb and drink thoroughly. I know that lawns perked up, shrubs and bushes found sustenance and trees absorbed every drop giving them all new life for days to come. It is amazing how much our world needs water. I am glad that our friends out west got some yesterday.

As part of my job responsibilities, I manage three recreational sports fields. Growing grass on those fields is paramount so that we are able to offer quality outdoor programs. Every year two of our three sports fields do wonderfully. On those fields the grass is always growing strong especially in the summer months when it is the hottest. We have enjoyed such strong stands of grass on those two surfaces mostly because of one thing. We have been able to irrigate.

Every week, except for the cold winter months, we cast at least an inch of water on two of our three fields. Having access to an ample water supply, a well planned piping system and a regulated electronic system, has lead to our fields being covered and green. This is all due to the fact that we have been able to deliver water to them on a regular basis.

Our third field, until very recently, has not operated in this fashion. Our third recreational sports field has never had an irrigation system. It has been strapped to the frequency of natural rainfall. This set up is fine if you have no concern about field surface quality but for a sports field a good stand of grass is critical. A good coverage of thick lush grass can only occur if you have a consistent source of water. Therefore, until very recently, our third field has never had the chance for a quality surface. Whatever seed we sowed and whatever sod we patched would never take hold because we could not guarantee a consistent application of life-giving water.

However, as of this past fall, this has all changed. We now have irrigation on our third field. We now have a consistent source of water and from now on we will not be held to the unpredictability of natural occurring rainfall. We are now able to plant and maintain grasses just like our other locations. Regular, consistent, irrigation will now give us the opportunity to have a field which can be all that it has the potential of being. We now have water.

I have a question for you all. Have you been getting water consistently into your life? No, I am not talking about drinking a bottle of Le Bleu water. I am talking about spiritual water. I am talking about whether you are receiving spiritual water on a regular basis. Through the irrigation system which the Lord has been built for you, I am asking whether or not you have taken advantage of what He has done for us. I am asking whether you have turned on the spiritual irrigation system which has tapped our Lord's unlimited supply of spiritual blessing. This supply has been given to us through a pipeline. His name is Jesus. I am asking whether you are accessing the spiritual water which gives us the needed sustenance to live this life successfully. When we do, our lives are healthy and strong spiritually. When we do receive water, we are like one of our irrigated sports fields. Our grass will be thick, green and strong to make it through life, especially the tough summer months.

Or, like we oftentimes do, are you leaving your life up to the random chances of rainfall? Are you setting your watering cycle to whenever spiritual opportunities happen to pass your way? Do you participate only if it super convenient?

Or, do you deliberately decide to engage in the watering of spiritual activities? Do you purposely make up your mind to have a personal prayer time, go to a bible study or even attend a worship service at a local church?

If we want our Lord's spiritual fruit in our lives, we must access the Source and pipeline which Jesus has built for us. We must make a conscious decision to turn on the water. If we want what our good Lord would have for us, we must turn on His watering irrigation system and receive the spiritual water which will nourish our souls. If we turn it on regularly, we will experience the Christian life which our Lord has promised all who come to Him. When we have access to this living water, we will never be spiritually thirsty again and will produce all that the Lord intends for us to produce.

The inspired word of the Lord speaks of this need for all of us to be planted by streams of this spiritual water. Psalm 1:1-3 says "Blessed is the man who does not walk in the counsel of the wicked or stand in the way of sinners or sit in the seat of mockers. But his delight is in the law of the Lord, and on his law he meditates day and night. He is like a tree planted by streams of water, which yields fruit in season and whose leaf does not wither. Whatever he does prospers."

Are you taking the necessary time to delight in God's word, the living stream of water? Are you pondering His promises and His presence both day and night? If you do, God's holy word says that you will be like a tree planted by streams of water, irrigated every day. If you turn on this irrigation system of spending time with the One who loves you and desires the best for you, you will bear fruit and you will find the success which the Lord desires for us to enjoy.

Galatians 5:22 "But the fruit of the spirit is love, joy, peace, patience, kindness, goodness, faithfulness, gentleness and self-control…"

Examine your life even this day and ask yourselves this question once again: are you receiving His living water? If you are, keep it up and keep going strong. If you have stepped back, I would like to encourage you to step back onto the field and turn on the water.

If you step back onto the field with the irrigation system running, you will move towards a life which our creator would have for you, an abundant life which is full and meaningful.

Scripture reading: John 7:37-38

As always, draw near to God and He will draw near to you.

The Mantel

My wife has been working steadily on our fireplace mantel for the past few days now. We picked out the mantel several weeks ago but now she has begun the long process of getting it ready for our living room area. The job is a difficult one in that she has to strip all of the old paint off the wood and fill in the gaps with wood filler before she can even begin to think about painting it. She has already gone through a couple pints of stripper and the sander cranked up this evening. I do believe that she is close to finishing this step but as she has found out, it is very difficult to get all of the paint off of the wood. With all of the tools, all of the chemicals and all of the elbow grease applied to the project, there is still some paint in areas that will just not come off.

I do not know the history of this mantel but I do believe that it has been a part of another family's living room in times past. It is a possibility that this mantel dates way back because of the many layers of paint which my wife has been working through. It seems like the previous owners painted it and then after sometime someone painted it again and then again. I think that this mantel may have been the part of a several homes because of the multiple layers discovered over these past few days. Layers have been built up over time on this mantel creating a real hardship to get back to the original wood. Because the previous owners did not sand to the wood but just painted over it, my wife's job is twice or even three times the work. It is quite a chore because of these extra layers. The old paint was never sanded clean. A new coat of paint was just applied on top of the old.

When we ignore sin in our lives and never confess them to our merciful Lord, we are doing what these previous owners did to this mantel. When we do not get rid of the old coat of disobedience in our lives and just cover it up, we are building up a life which is getting more and more calloused and layered to the things of God. When we paint layer after layer of a wandering heart onto our lives and never get sanded clean, we get further away from the life our loving Lord wants to give us.

However, when we come to the Lord Jesus, we too begin like this mantel. We have layers of paint from lives which have oftentimes run from the Lord. There are chips and uneven areas from days, weeks, months and possibly years of wear and tear. Then the Lord Jesus begins His call into our lives. He calls out to us promising to make us new. He speaks to us through His Word telling us that no matter what our life has been like, no matter what we have done, no matter how many layers of life paint that we have covered ourselves with, He can completely wash us clean and give us a new look. This new look is not a new coat of paint on the outside but a new mantel, with new wood built again from the inside out.

How are you living your life these days? Are you living each day realizing you have been given a new life, a new mantel because of Jesus Christ and His finished work on the cross? When you wake up in the mornings, are getting ready to set out to school or work and are preparing to put your hands to whatever is in front of you, do you realize the gift that you have been given in Christ? Do you know that you have been blessed with every spiritual blessing in the heavenly places? Do you realize that the Lord Jesus has given you a new heart? Do you realize the great privilege it is not to have a layered life with coats of paint building up year after year? Do you know that all of this came at a great price, the price of our savior giving His life for us? If you realize this each and every day; if you acknowledge this before the Lord and thank Him each and every day; then you are right where you need to be. If you are aware that your spiritual position has been cleansed from sin and made new, then you are poised to make an impact on a watching world.

However, if you do not realize all of this, are rarely thankful and continue to layer sin onto your life, you will realize someday that no matter how hard you try, no matter how many chemicals you apply or sanders you purchase, you will never find new life. New life is found only in the Lord Jesus Christ. In Him and only in Him can we receive a new mantel because striving to do it ourselves does not work.

Ephesians 2:8-10 says "For by grace you have been saved through faith, and that not of yourselves; it is a gift of God, not of works lest anyone should boast. For we are His workmanship created in Christ Jesus for good works prepared beforehand that we should walk in them."

Matthew 11:28 Jesus speaking, "Come to Me, all you who labor and are heavy laden, and I will give you rest. Take my yoke upon you and learn from Me, for I am gentle and lowly in heart, and you will find rest for your souls."

I John 1:9 says "If we confess our sins, He is faithful and just to forgive us our sins and cleanse us from all unrighteousness."

If you are still layering with paint; I would encourage you to go a different direction. Go to the one who cannot only cleanse you from all of that old paint but will give you a new mantel freshly built with new wood.

He is there even as you read this at this moment. Call out to Him. He is waiting. He is willing. He loves you more than we will ever know.

Scripture reading: Isaiah 1:18

Draw near to God and He will draw near to you.

Voices

There is a book entitled, *The Road Less Traveled* which begins with this statement: "Life is hard." If you live long enough and put yourself out there enough, you too will agree with that statement. Life is indeed hard. We know this not because we have a ditch to dig every day or a mountain to climb with a hundred pound pack on our backs. No, we know this because oftentimes there are things which come into our life which stops us in our tracks and causes us to rethink everything. In my own life I have had two or three moments which have forced me to stop like that. I have had things come my way which has caused me to ponder the big issues of life. For many reading my words this day, this may have happened to you this week. For many of you, you may have very recently been forced to pull over to the side of the road and turn off the car. For many of you, you may have gotten through the day but only after uttering the words to yourself, "Life is hard."

Whenever I walk into a room filled with people, I absorb a few things all related to my senses. Even though there are several other senses, hearing seems to be one of my most cherished. Sometimes I get to hear music playing. At other times I may hear dishes clanging in a kitchen. Or, like in a setting in which I am very familiar, I may hear basketballs bouncing, weights clanging or feet stomping on the floor in unison. However, in most every place which I step into, there is one thing which is always present when there are people together. I hear voices. I hear the voices of people talking to one another.

Sometimes these voices are spoken loudly. Other times they are uttered quietly only being heard by the one in closest proximity. Sometimes these voices are spoken wrapped in a sea of laughter. Other times the words are hesitantly spoken cracking slightly because of sorrowful emotion attached to it. Sometimes the words lifted from these voices are expressed with confusion. Other times the words and voices are spoken with comfort and understanding. I walked into a room a couple days ago and heard all of these kinds of voices.

Every day we are exposed to voices. These voices can come from a person sitting across the table from us, from a person teaching us from the front of a classroom or they can come from within. These voices can come from other people's talk or they can come from our own self-talk. Voices may be actual life philosophies shared from the mouth of a speaker or they can come indirectly from the expectations and pressures of culture. They can come from a group which we are affiliated with or even from family. As you know, these voices can be positive, filled with words of hope, words of optimism and words of comfort. Or, these voices can be negative voices filled with words of despair, words of hopelessness and words of aloneness.

The Holy Bible addresses this topic of voices and words head on. God's word goes toe to toe with the issue of these voices and counters it with the counsel from the mind of our Creator. As you know, The Lord's voice is the ultimate game plan for life, the victorious play book and the true operating manual. The Lord's voice as shared in His word, is His architectural drawings, His blueprints and His step by step directions on how to live life. All that He says addresses the voices which need to be loudest in our mental room of life. He promises that if we let His voice be loudest in our lives, that we will be able to live life to the fullest and appropriately handle the challenging problems and issues of life in the best way possible.

Here are some verses which address our thinking, the words which need to be heard in our inner conversation.

"Whatever is pure, whatever is lovely, whatever is righteous, whatever is praiseworthy, whatever is excellent, think on these things." Philippians 4:8

"Let no wholesome word come out of your mouth except that which is good for edification according to the need of the moment, that it may benefit the hearers." Ephesians 4:29

"Let your conversation always be with grace seasoned with salt, so that you may know how you should respond to each person." Colossians 4:6

"Speak truthfully one to another." "Confess your sins to one another." "Encourage one another."

And "Life and death are in the power of the tongue." - Proverbs 18:21

Per this last verse in Proverbs, there are life words and there are death words spoken every day. In classrooms, at dinner tables and in individual minds all across our world, words are being spoken which are either life words or death words. They can come from another person or can come from within.

Life voices or life words are words which bring healing, hope and a future. Such words motivate and inspire can-do spirits, cause individuals to pursue excellence and put greatness within our grasp. We all need these kinds of words. We all need these kinds of voices to be spoken to us every day. They give us the opportunity to ponder and act upon their rich truth in our own lives. When correctly spoken, such voices give meaning, purpose and direction to our lives. Life is truly in the power of the tongue.

Conversely, the bible says that death words are in the power of the tongue as well. All across our country death words are being spoken. In classrooms, in residence halls, in car rides and in individual minds, there are death words being heard and absorbed. Such voices push us to give up, give in and to think the worst. These voices can take us down a path which none of us want to go.

So I ask you this very day, what kind of voices are you letting into your mind? What kind of voices are you speaking into the lives of others? What kind of words are you speaking into those whom you love? Are you building up instilling hope and a future? Or, are you constantly being negative and critical to those in your world? What kind of self-talk do you bathe your mind with every day? Is it based on pop-culture or is it mined from the stone of Truth found in the mind of the master architect? Where do you find your words when you utter them to yourself and others? Do you pull them from someone else's idea bank or do you get it from the Author of Life itself?

The voices or words we choose to follow will lead us in a direction in life. One direction will be a path of joy, of purpose, of love and of positive impact. Other words will lead us down paths but not necessarily the best path that the Lord has for us. Remember Jesus said, "I am the way, the truth and the life…" His voice is the one which will lead us where we need to go.

Are you ready for such a journey? Are you ready to go God's way and not follow the voices of our culture? Are you ready to be a vessel who communicates and thinks words which the Lord God Almighty asks us to think? We need the right words in our lives. We need the right voices to be heard.

Start even this day to listen to our Lord's voice. Start even this day to share the Lord's voice/words with yourself and with those you love. Start even this day to drown out those voices which go against everything good that the Lord would have for us. You are where you are for a reason. Go and be the person the Lord God Almighty would have you be. Yes. Life is hard and at times very hard. However, it is possible to live life abundantly if we only listen to the right voice.

Scripture reading: Psalm 119:105

As always, draw near to God and He will draw near to you.

Diamonds on the Street

Several weeks back I attended a conference in San Diego, California. On one of the nights at the conference, I took the advice of a friend and went to a diner renowned for its hamburgers. Since I did not know of any other dining establishments, I decided to take her up on the suggestion. After driving around the block several times trying to find a parking place, I finally found one about a quarter mile away from my dinner destination, Hodads.

I walked into Hodad's, picked up a well worn laminated menu at the counter and found a seat. After looking over the menu and making my choice, a 1/3 pound bacon cheese burger and a side of frings (potato fries and onion rings), I panned the room looking for indicators as to why this place was on my friend's suggestion list. All of the things that I look for in a restaurant were not present. In fact, all of the things which I observed were in direct opposition to what I normally look for in a place to eat.

Instead of waiters dressed in uniforms matching the company brand, neatly groomed with a notepad in hand, I had a guy in regular street clothes, ball cap on backwards and nodding when I made my order. Instead of squeaky clean table cloth covering the tables, I had a wooden stool and a wooden table to eat on. Instead of soothing classical music or possibly some soft jazz playing over the speaker system, I had heavy metal pumping in the background. Instead of being surrounded with people who looked like me, I was surrounded by individuals from all walks of life ranging from pony tails, to rings in noses, to couples, to all races and life position. What I saw on the outside did not match what was to eventually arrive at my table in just a few minutes.

Even later that night what I was going to experience was not going to match what I saw on the outside as well.

When my server stopped with the basket of frings, I can honestly say that the onion rings and steak fries were some of the best that I had ever eaten. Nevertheless, it paled in comparison to the hamburger that showed up next. The hamburger was not only huge but it was tasty topped with a fresh onion, tomatoes and lettuce. Everything about the meal was outstanding. It blew past the hamburger joints of In and Out, Cook Out and even Five Guys in my estimation. The impression that I had when I arrived was totally changed when I walked out the front door. I walked in skeptical and questioning the recommendation only to leave having been won over by what came out of the kitchen. What was foreign to me on the outside was set aside as I am now a fan of Hodad's Burgers. My meal did not match my premature expectation. As I was soon going to find out on my walk to my car, my expectation of other things was not going to match as well.

Since the meal was much more than I could eat, I asked for a carryout box for the remaining steak fries and onion rings. Looking forward to possibly a late night snack, I bagged them up not knowing that these leftovers would find another home in just a few minutes.

After crossing the street at the stop light, I turned to make the quarter mile walk to my car. I began walking up the sidewalk and noticed about 50 yards up a man sitting on the sidewalk with his back against the wall. With it being late evening I knew who the guy was. I knew that he was probably going to be a homeless guy maybe looking for a hand out. I had my leftovers and I was set for the night. I did not know this guy and I was determined to walk past quickly so I could get on with my business.

81

As I came parallel to this homeless individual I noticed that he appeared to be in his late 20's. I continued to glance over at him and realized that he did not attempt to raise his head. He kept his head down just fiddling with some of his belongings. He appeared to be ashamed of his situation and did not want to be noticed really at all. What I had expected from this guy was an interruption, embarrassment and possibly confrontation. All I got was the sight of a man who was broken, needy and probably hungry. At that moment, in total opposition to what I had intended to do, I stopped and spoke to the young man. I said, "Hey bud. Do you want some food?" Slowly lifting his head he said, "Yes. I would." As I sat the food down in front of him, I turned to go but something stopped me. I decided to ask him one more question. I asked, "What is your story? Why are you here?" With an extremely open demeanor, he then proceeded to tell me where he was from, what his struggles have been and why he was on the streets. For the next ten minutes or so, I spoke with a man who I expected to be one way from a distance only to have my point of view changed when he was in front of me.

You see, when I took the time to stop, lend a hand with a bag of food and ask for his story, I found a friend. I found a young man who had struggles, continually felt like giving up and felt like he was unworthy, unfit and unable to find happiness. As you know, all of that is untrue. There is a way, there is a person who can enter a person's life and give him a fresh hope and a new start. In fact, there is a person who can wash all of his past sins away. There is a person, no matter what our station in life, who can give us eternal life and a place in God's home some day.

As I listened to my friend, I then told him about Jesus. I told him that He loves him more than he can imagine. I told him that He died for him and wants to wash his sins away giving him access to God's presence and all of His spiritual blessings. I told him to consider Jesus. I told him that Jesus knows his situation, that He knows his struggles and that He knows his fears. In fact, He knows everything about him and yet, He loves him more than he could ever imagine. As I turned to go I said this, "Bud, if you decide to accept Jesus into your life and to accept his forgiveness, I will see you again someday." I turned and continued my walk to the car, praying for this man, praying that he would turn to Jesus.

What I expected when I walked up to Hodad's was changed when I walked out. In similar fashion, what I expected when I walked by my friend on the street changed as I drove away. After that day I now have a burger place that rivals my favorites. And more importantly, I now may have a friend who I will see again someday.

My challenge to you this day, going into this coming week is this: Look beyond the stools in the restaurant, look beyond the heads bowed low on the sidewalk, look and see what the Lord God almighty sees. When looking at people, look past the outside and care for them, meet their needs, ask for their story and then most of all tell them the greatest story ever told. Tell them the story of God coming down in human form, dying on a cross, only to be resurrected on the third day, forgiving sins and making a pathway into His presence for all of those who will put their faith and trust in Him.

Tell this story to yourself and then tell this story to those who need to hear it. Then you can walk away knowing this: No matter what happens you will see them again someday.

Scripture reading: John 1:12

Draw near to God and He will draw near to you.

The Tin Man

For many homes across our land, Christmas morning is an exciting time for the entire family. On Christmas morning we too in the Floyd house get pretty pumped up. Along with the anticipation of the day, we have several traditions which we eagerly go through every year. One of the traditions that we do is that on Christmas morning, after everyone has finally woken up, we gather around the family room and listen to the reading of Luke chapter 2, the Christmas story. While listening to the story, my wife brings out another family tradition, a warm tray of freshly baked cinnamon rolls. After the story is read and the rolls are eaten, it is time to open presents.

In our home, most every year, each child gets three main gifts. The three gifts are in remembrance of the quantity of gifts which Jesus received from the wise men. He received three gifts: gold, frankincense and myrrh so each one of the children receives three as well. However, before we get to the three main gifts, my wife gives each one of the children one additional thing. She hands out their stocking. Inside each stocking are a series of little gifts. The gifts range from movies, to socks, to chocolates to ornaments. My wife and I also have a stocking as well. This year my wife stuffed my stocking with something which jumped my heart several beats when I pulled it out. My wife got me an album. The album was the greatest hits collection from a group called America. I was grinning ear to ear and have been listening to it on long car rides ever since.

America is a soft rock group which gained fame in the mid 70's with hit songs such as "A Horse with No Name", "Ventura Highway", "Daisy Jane" and "Sister Golden Hair." However, one of my favorite songs which they sang was a song called "The Tin Man." Though America was known for many nonsensical lines in their music, there is one line from "The Tin Man" which makes much sense. The song rings true to me every time I hear and begin to hum it. Every time I hear this one phrase, I am reminded of something that is so true. Every time I sing it to myself, my mind drifts to such a deep truth that I desire to recall it as often as I can in my everyday life. The line goes like this: "Oz never did give nothing to the Tin man, that he didn't, didn't already have."

For those of us who can recall the movie called, "The Wizard of Oz", we know that the wizard really didn't do or give the Lion, the Scarecrow or the Tin Man anything new at all. He just told them what they already had but that they had never realized. For the Tin Man, at the end of the movie he received a heart shaped ticking watch. This was to remind him that he really did have a heart after all. When I think of the Tin Man, I am reminded of something which I already have as well. I am reminded of the truth of a possession that I have already received. This possession is something which I need to be constantly reminded of as well. This gift is not given by the Wizard of Oz in the Land of Oz but from the Lord God Almighty Himself. This possession is explained in Holy Scripture. It is found in the first chapter of Ephesians. In this most treasured of texts, there is something which I have received that I do not need to go looking for any longer. There is something that I already have. There is something that I have already been given, never to be added to. It is all that I will ever need.

Ephesians 1:3 says "Blessed be the God and Father of our Lord Jesus Christ who has blessed us with every spiritual blessing in the heavenly places in Christ."

You see, those of us who have believed in Jesus have every spiritual blessing available to mankind. We have everything that we need right at this moment to live the life which we have in front of us. If we have accepted Jesus Christ, he has packed us with every spiritual blessing possible. He has equipped us to live fruitful, productive and influential Christian lives. Because of these spiritual blessings, we are able to live victoriously making a real difference in the world. There is not another blessing to be received at another time. There is not another aha moment that we must wait for. Jesus Christ has given us every piece of spiritual armor, weaponry, and gifts that are at his disposal. He has blessed us with every spiritual blessing in the heavenly places. Though there are many others, some of these include: the Holy Spirit, Holy Scripture, your calling and of course your spiritual gift. You have everything you need. Once you accept Jesus Christ as your savior, you are a power packed individual loaded to the hilt with every spiritual blessing available.

So my question now is this: What are you doing with it? Are you letting your spiritual blessings sit idly on the sidelines of life when we need you in the game? Are you using your spiritual gifts to make yourself and others better, stronger and more encouraged? Do you realize that the Lord Himself has given you everything that you need to able to attack each and every day? Are you reading the spiritually rich words of the Lord? If needed, are you confessing your time on the sideline and will you ask Him to help you to get back into the game, using His complete game plan?

Take time even this day to start the week off on a great note. Thank the Lord God almighty for blessing you with every spiritual blessing in the heavenlies. Ask Him to show you this coming week how you can be a positive light in your world. Ask Him to unearth the spiritual blessings placed in your life so as to glorify Him and please Him in all that you say and do.

Then after a semester, after a year, after a dozen years, after a lifetime of acknowledging and using the gifts given to us, we may all hear from the Lord those words we all should long to hear, "Well done, good and faithful servant."

It is never too late. You can be and do what you were created to be and do. Start this day to use all of those blessings which He went to the cross to provide for us. I am pulling for you all. You have what it takes. You possess what you need.

"Oz never did nothing to the Tin Man, that he didn't, didn't already have."

I am a Tin Man. I have it. If you are a Tin Man, you do as well.

Let's go on this great adventure together and invite as many as will come to join us. It is well worth it.

Scripture reading: Colossians 2:10

Draw near to God and He will draw near to you.

A Place in Line, A Place at Home

With my two daughters next to me and my son-in-law shoulder to shoulder, I did something a couple nights ago that I had not done since my pre-teen years in Alaska. Though I hate to admit it, I got in line one hour early to see a movie. Yes I know, why would I do such a thing? With theatres all across town and movies offered on the hour, why would I get in line one hour early? The reason was the fact that if we did not get there early enough, we might not be able to get a good seat. If we did not get there in advance, we might be relegated to the front row thus causing a kink in our necks for who knows how long. If we did not wait in line for at least an hour, not only will we miss the good seats, we may be separated and not able to sit together at all.

Upon arriving at the theatre, we claimed spots number 11 through number 14 in line. Because of our early arrival, we were confident that we would get prime seats at the movie that we were all looking forward to attending. In an hour we would be able to see Katnis Everdeen battle for survival in *Hunger Games 2 – Catching Fire*.

When the doors opened and the rush to the open seats began, we knew we would have our pick of the theatre. When I yelled, "Let's go!" we ran right behind the ten darting teenagers in front of us and found four seats center row about half way up the auditorium. As we ran, acting like youngsters half our age, we were all laughing about our mad dash to our seats as well as the joyful anticipation of the movie ahead of us. Getting a ticket early in the day, getting to the front of the line and gaining access to an anticipated movie was well worth it. We received an opportunity to get a great seat, viewed an exciting film and sat alongside family who I love dearly. I enjoyed every second that I spent with family at Hunger Games 2. It was wonderful.

As you can imagine, the line grew and grew wrapping the entire lobby before reaching the entrance door. I think there were close to two hundred people in line. As I think about that special evening, I am reminded of another line in which all of us someday we will be asked to stand.

This line which I am referring to will be a line formed with people from all walks of life. There will be family members, friends from school or work, acquaintances from our community and strangers from possibly miles away. Those in this line will also be waiting for the opening of a set of doors. The doors opening in front of this line will open to a theatre room so wonderful that it will exceed anything we could think or imagine. Not only will the surroundings in this theatre be breathtaking, there will be people who will be eagerly awaiting all who are entering next.

When the doors are opened at this theatre, just like the other day, there will also be a ticket taker. The ticket taker will be the person who will approve access into this wonderful space. However, instead of tearing every ticket of every person in line, the ticket taker will be looking for one unique ticket which will allow entrance. The ticket taker will be looking for a ticket which has a special stamp on it. The stamp will be in the shape of a cross, stamped in a man's blood with a word imprinted at the bottom of the cross. The word will be 'forgiven.' As this ticket taker greets each person desiring to enter in, the ticket taker will take the ticket from each person, will look to see if it is the one which says 'forgiven' on it and then will proceed to look each one in the eye. He will look them in the eye and will say to those with the special ticket, "I know you. We have a friendship. You have obeyed me. You have loved me. You have trusted me with your life. Come on in and enjoy something which I have prepared for you since the beginning of time."

As the line moves toward the entrance to the theatre, each person will be stopped and checked for the right ticket. Some will have stamps on them that say other things and do not have the cross, the blood and the word 'forgiven' on it. Some will say, 'Made lots of money', others will say, 'Gave things to the poor', others will say 'Didn't smoke, drink or cuss very much' and still others will say 'I did religious activities.' Each one of these individuals will hand their ticket over to the ticket taker and He will look at it. With loving and yet righteous eyes, He will say something like this, "I never knew you. You rejected the love offering of forgiveness in the Son Jesus Christ. There is no cleansing of your sins from the Son's death and resurrection. This ticket that you have crafted yourself does not have the stamp that I approve. Yes, they are works but I never knew you and you never knew me personally. You must now leave. You must turn around and join those in the other theatre; the theatre over there. It does not have sound. It does not have joyful company. It does not have beauty. It does not have the presence of the One whose blood is on the stamp. You made your choice prior to getting in line. You chose to follow another way and not The Way, The Truth and The Life."

As you know, the ticket taker will be Jesus Christ himself. He made the movie, the movie theatre and the great adventure which will be for those who turn to Him in faith. He decided what type of ticket which will allow access into His presence in heaven. He will be the one at the door some day.

God's word speaks of this theatre and the ticket required to get in. The place which all believers will enjoy some day:

John 14:1-3, 6 "Let not your heart be troubled; you believe in God, believe also in Me. In My Father's house are many mansions; if it were not so, I would have told you. I go to prepare a place for you. And if I go and prepare a place for you, I will come again and receive you to Myself; that where I am there you may be also.

vs. 6 Jesus said to him, "I am the way, the truth and the life. No one comes to the Father except through me."

Revelation 21:3, 4 ... "Behold, the tabernacle of God is with men, and He will dwell with them and they shall be His people. God Himself will be their God. And God will wipe away every tear from their eyes; there will be no more death, nor sorrow, nor crying. There shall be no more pain, for the former things have passed away."

I Thessalonians 4:13 "But I do not want you to be ignorant brethren, concerning those who have fallen asleep, lest you sorrow as others who have no hope. For if we believe that Jesus died and rose again, even so God will bring with Him those who sleep in Jesus."

When we die, we will all be asked to stand in line. Some day we will all stand before the ticket taker. It will be Jesus. Someday we will enter into paradise or not. Do you know for sure that you will get in? Do you know for sure that you will have a seat and a place in the theatre of God? If you are not sure, ask Him to be your savior even this very day. If you are not sure, believe on Him and accept Him as your Lord and savior. He wants everyone in line to enter in. He wants you and He wants me. Someday I may see you guys in line with me.

I am going to hold up my ticket high. When I see you, I do hope that you will have it as well.

Scripture reading: I John 5:12

As always, draw near to God and He will draw near to you.

Scales in Our Lives

The Grand Finale of the television series called The Biggest Loser came down to three individuals the other night. One of the final two individuals lost 222 pounds or 52% of his body weight after originally tipping the scales at 409. His final tally on the scales measured 187 pounds. The lady who won the competition, Rachel Fredrickson lost even more. She lost 155 pounds or 59.62% of her starting bodyweight. She was 260 pounds. She is now 105. As it stands today, she is also the all time record-holder for the highest percentage of body weight ever lost on the show. The record was 55% but now because of her efforts it is nearly 60%.

These individuals are not alone in this battle to return to a healthy body weight. In fact, obesity is a huge problem in the United States. Trust for America's Health and The Robert Wood Johnson foundations say that 13 States have obesity rates above 30% of their population. 41 states have obesity rates of at least 25%. Colorado has the least amount of adults in their population tipping the scales at 20.5%. Louisiana tops the list of having the most obese people residing in the state. 34.7% are clinically obese.

Based on further research, The Robert Wood Johnson foundation says that nearly a third of children and adolescents in the United States are overweight or obese as well. That is more than 23 million kids and teenagers.

As you can imagine, obesity is a problem that not only increases the chances of sickness over one's lifetime, but it also increases the chance of a shortened life. How does this happen? How does this ever happen to a life? How does an individual gain so much weight? Some would say that it is a lack of access to facilities and programs which engage people. Others would state that individuals lack the monies to properly shop for healthy foods. And still others would comment that it is a lack of knowledge about what foods are high in calories and which ones are better for us. It is indeed all of the above.

How is this issue ever to be solved in a person's life? As the Biggest Loser shows, it can be solved by a few key things. First of all, there needs to be a real desire to lose weight. Great coaches also need to come alongside encouraging those in the difficulty to be eating right and to fill their life with lots of activity and exercise. The energy imbalance must somehow be shifted from consuming more calories to burning more and consuming less. Motivation, accountability, proper diet and regular exercise are the answers.

So I ask you this day, how does the scale look in your life? When you step onto it, does it depict a life that has shown a proper energy balance? Or, like me this week, is it showing that a change is in order?

How about the spiritual scale that you step onto each morning? When you step onto it, is it revealing a balance of energy expenditure and consumption? Energy wise, have you been making a sincere effort to exercise your spiritual muscles, burning away unwanted thoughts and habits and replacing them with wonderful, beautiful mindsets? Are your spiritual muscles lean and strong and able to endure the competition and spiritual battles which surface each day? Or, are they flabby needing a shaping up?

Consumption wise, have you been eating the right amount of healthy spiritual food each day? Or, have you been eating lots of junk food because it is so convenient? In other words, are you daily drinking the pure Words from our Lord? Or, is your mind only focused on your world, your circumstances and the sways of pop culture? A spiritually strong life eats right and exercises the faith often.

Jesus said that He is the bread of life. Jesus said that He is the living water. Jesus said that if we sit at His table and consume what He has for us then we will never thirst and never grow hungry spiritually.

I do hope that none of you have to deal with the physical weight problems of those on The Biggest Loser. But more than that, I pray that each and every one of you will not let the spiritual energy consumption be so out of balance that you become flabby spiritually. Exercise your spiritual muscles daily. Eat and drink fully from the pure milk and meat of God's Word daily. And then, every once in a while, step up onto a spiritual scale and ask another whom you respect spiritually to read your scale. No, there will not be a number up on the scale to read. No, there will not be a percentage lost. The scale will measure spiritual maturity and strength. This scale will measure spiritual maturity if we have been eating right and exercise has been commonplace. If it reads mature, it will bring a smile onto the face of the One who weighs everything in His balance, the Lord God Almighty.

Some of the things that this scale may read may include: Shows love for others especially the household of the faith. Trusts and obeys the Lord's leading, no matter where it points. Experiences joy, peace, patience, kindness, goodness and self-control. Is not overcome with evil but overcomes evil with good. Prays to the Lord about all things, no matter how big or how small. Works hard and is an example to others by his life, in love, in faith and in faithfulness.

Is ready at all times to give a reason for the hope that he has. Lives a life which reveals a Love for the One who gave His life for him.

Thanks for your partnership in this wonderful journey. See you on the scales.

Scripture reading: James 2:20

Draw near to God and He will draw near to you.

What I Thought Was Good Was Bad

I played some basketball this past week and I had a hard time getting around the floor. I could not make a cut in any direction. I could not make any east - west moves thus having to play straight ahead. I tried cleaning my shoes but my shoes were not the problem. I considered dusting the floor but dirt on the surface was not the problem. The problem was with the floors themselves. The problem had nothing to do with what was tracked in by previous players. The problem had to do with how we had been cleaning the floors.

For years, many years, we have been using a floor cleaning machine on our wooden gym floors. From the beginning, we were told to use one or two cups of the bright shine solution when using the floor scrubber. The problem was that this was wrong. We should never had been putting so much solution in with the water. The machine was basically working against us. Instead of floating the dirt and vacuuming it up into the holding tank, our floor scrubber was putting down a layer of film every time that we did the floors. Every week and month after month, we had been contributing to the problem. We were creating a slick surface instead of gaining a clean, squeaking floor which all basketball players love to play on. What we thought was good was in fact bad for our floors. What we thought was taking care of the problem was in fact creating a bigger problem for us. Who would of thought?

This past week we brought in a floor consultant and he told us what we needed to be doing. He brought his crew to the gym last night and spent two hours mopping the floors. If his first efforts did not work, he was going to use a vinegar and water solution to cut through the film. The scrubber will then get new pads and the solution applied will be cut substantially. What we thought was good was in fact bad. What a lesson that we had to learn. I am excited about the future but saddened that the court experience has been less then it could have been.

How about you? Like me, have you been doing something or thinking in a way that you think is good? Stop for a minute, take an inventory, rethink your position, re-evaluate your actions, and review your direction. Why? Because just like me, what you are doing to your floors may be wrong. What I thought was good was in fact making it worse. What you are doing may be in fact making things worse.

So how do we get it right? How do we make sure that we are living life as it is supposed to be lived? How do we know that we are treating others as they are supposed to be treated? How do we know that we are pursuing the things that we should be pursing? How do we know that we are thinking on the things that should be thought upon? How do we know that we too will not be in fact adding a film of solution onto our life only making things worse? There is an answer. There is a master consultant. There is one who made the floors of your life. There is one who knows how to take care of our situations. There is one who knows how to keep us functioning at the highest level possible. He knows what to do. He knows you and what is best. He knows me and knows what is best for me. I just need to follow His lead. I just need to listen to His instructions on how to take care of my floors, my life.

If you are interested in hearing from the Master's life manual, if you are interested in discussing how His guidelines for being all that we are capable of becoming, then open up His playbook, the Holy Bible and read deeply. Think on the things that are said. Apply every principle, every precept, every call and you know what? Your floor will be optimum making a difference in multiple lives who cross your path. It is possible to be and do what we have been created to be and do.

II Timothy 3:16 says "All scripture is inspired by God useful for teaching, rebuking, correcting and training in righteousness, so that the man of God may be thoroughly equipped for every good work."

Keep seeking. Keep listening. Keep getting it right. Don't be fooled into thinking what is bad is good. Our loving Lord has the plan. His promises are true. His promises are always correct, always spot on and always for our good.

Scripture reading: I John 5:3

Draw near to God and He will draw near to you.

Only When It Works For Me

Every morning about 7:35am my youngest son and I head off to school. Since he is not yet able to drive himself to school, I get to take him. His school is only 10 minutes away from home so I can drop him off and most of the time make it in to work just a few minutes after 8am. Many times the drive is conversational going over the things of the day. Other times it is kind of quiet because of a looming test facing him and every minute needs to be spent in review. Nevertheless, most of the time the ride ends with a few statements that I make to my youngest son as I drop him off. Many times I tell him to be salt and light. Most of the time I remind him to work hard, be a good friend and to be respectful. Then I try to add one additional thing to my parting words. I tell him that I will strive to the same.

As I pulled out of the drop off zone in front of the school a few mornings back this 'striving to do the same' statement came face to face with real life. Though a very simple example, what I experienced challenged me on whether I am indeed striving to do the same in all areas of my life as well.

I pulled out into the main road car and there was a line of cars 25 deep. Car after car stacked up bumper to bumper waiting for the intersection light to change just a quarter mile ahead. However, as most of us know who frequent this process, there is a turn lane in the middle of the street. The turn lane makes a two way street three lanes wide. This turn lane is there beginning at the bottom of the hill but the legal access to it only becomes available near the top of the hill. At the top of the hill the double yellow line opens up to all of those who have been waiting patiently in line to access it. When it opens is when it is legal to use the center lane.

Most mornings I am ahead of schedule arriving early to work 20 to 30 minutes. That morning it was different. I needed to stop by the barber shop on the way in to work. Instead of having a buffer of time, it was going to be close to get to my desk on time. So there I was waiting in line feeling a little anxious for I was shortened for time. There was a turn lane just feet away staring at me. I could eliminate the wait if I used it. I could be at the light in 30 seconds. I would be first in line for the left turn signal. I could be ahead of the long line and off towards the barber shop. It was also illegal to use it.

Most every morning, I sit in line and wait for the double yellow to open up and then merge to the center turn lane when it is legal to do so. Most every morning, I am ahead of schedule and can be relaxed and wait patiently for my turn. During my time in line, car after car have come blowing past me using the center lane to get ahead of the pack, just as I was considered doing that morning. In fact I have seen a couple accidents that have happened because of cars turning legally when the double yellow comes open only to be sideswiped by one speedily coming up from behind. When I am ahead of schedule, many times I have a 'holier than thou" mindset. Because of my obedience to the traffic laws, I find myself thinking, "It is the law to wait until I am allowed to turn left. I am obeying the laws of the land and I am just a wonderful example of a law abiding citizen." That reasoning left me that one morning. I found out in only a few seconds that I had been saying that only 'when it worked for me.'

Because I was in a hurry and had to get the barber shop soon, I pulled out of the line, crossed over into the turn lane.

Disregarding my mindset when not pressed, I sped up through the center lane and got to the turn signal far ahead of the pack.

As I sat there in line, it suddenly dawned on me that all of those times that I sat in obedience and followed the traffic laws of that street were all just a show. All of that time, I was only obedient because it was working for me. I stayed in line and waited my time to turn only because I was not in a hurry. I did what I needed to do only because it was convenient and worked in my schedule.

As I sat at that intersection, being convicted of my actions, I then asked another question which I would like to ask you all this day. I asked myself, do I treat my walk with my Lord, my Christianity in the same way? Do I only obey when it works for me? Do I only follow Him when it is convenient for me? Do I only seek after Him when I have lots of time to do so? Do I only stand up for what is right when there are no other things going in my life? Do I only walk with my merciful, powerful, loving, faithful and all-wise, omniscient, all-knowing Heavenly Father when it works for me?

All too often the answer to these questions are 'yes'. Yes, I do only walk with Him when it works for me. I am not willing to sacrifice my time. I am not willing to sacrifice what others may think of me. I am not willing to sacrifice and to really do what I know I should be doing. Why not? Though there may be several reasons, one is that my walk with the Lord is not seen as a relationship but only as a list of do's and don'ts. Also, I am just too busy. I am not willing to take the time to walk with my Lord and engage in the needed Christian disciplines.

Such disciplines that are neglected may include: a daily prayer time, a daily time in the Word, a time of fellowship and bible study with other Christians, a time of talking of faith with others and going to a local church where youngsters and older folks would be encouraged by my presence.

I do not do any of it because it is just not convenient. It just is not able to fit into my schedule. It just is not working for me. I have to get to the barbershop you know. Yes, I know it is the right thing to do but right now it just isn't working for me. I will do it when it does work for me, when it is convenient, when the time is right, when all of the stars align.

I have been there. In fact, the temptation is still there for me each and every day. I can do this walk with the Lord thing when it is convenient or you know what? I can do it no matter what the circumstances. I urge you all to begin again. I implore you to start or continue down the path of a moment by moment, daily walk with the Lord no matter how late, or how on time your life circumstances are. Begin again to make the relationship with your Lord a priority of every day no matter how busy or how inconvenient it may be. He is waiting for you. He is wanting to be your closest friend, your wisest counselor, your source of power and strength and your loving Heavenly Father. He is not a to-do list. Reach out to Him in every arena of life. Involve Him in every decision. Look for His leading in every endeavor. And obey His prompting no matter how many cars are ahead of you in line. If you do, your way will be accompanied by the One who spoke life into existence, who will never leave you nor forsake you, who will give you true purpose and true joy for your entire life. Start today and I promise you that you will never regret it.

Will you blow it as I did? Yes, but He always takes us back and is willing to continue to shape us into the person we were born to become.

Scripture reading: I Timothy 4:12

Draw near to God and He will draw near to you.

Life Coins

Fifty people were in the room that day. When the group leader asked each one of us to step forward and share a hobby, Alex thought for sure that no one else in the room would step forward and join him. He had shared his hobby many times in many locations over the years and no one had ever shared the same love which he enjoyed. On that day Alex said that he was a numismatist. Every person stayed in their place except one person. Unknown to Alex, there was another person in the room who loved to collect coins as well. There was another who started collecting coins at the age of 9 and has had a collection ever since. Alex stepped forward and I joined him shouting out, "I have a 1932 D George Washington Quarter. We need to talk." From that point on, when our paths cross, the sharing of our coins has always been in the topic of conversation.

So what is so intriguing about collecting coins? What is the attraction in a hobby which continues to draw people from far and wide going to coin shows in order to buy, sell and collect coins? What is this hobby all about?

Though not an expert by any means, I believe that there are a few key draws to coin collecting. First of all, it is the idea that you have in your hands coins which were made during World War II, World War I or even in the 1800's. Just knowing that you have in your possession something which was possibly in the pockets of those from an earlier era is fun to think about. It may have been held by your great grandfather, Henry Ford, Albert Einstein, Thomas Edison, or possibly John D Rockefeller.

Coin collecting continues its intrigue when you realize that you only have a coin of a certain year. You may have the year on the coin but nothing before or after that date. You may also only have a coin made at a certain location but not at the others. You may have one cut at the Denver mint but not at the one made at the San Francisco mint. You may have the 1932 D (Denver) but not the 1932 (S) San Francisco. Holding an old coin in your hand is enjoyable and it is even more so when the coin is valuable. Possessing an old and valuable coin is the pinnacle of collecting coins.

What makes a coin valuable? A coin is valuable mostly because of two major things. It is valuable because of its age and its condition. A coin cut in 2012 which is in extra fine condition is not as valuable as a coin which was made in 1909 and is in extra fine condition. Age and condition make it valuable. When they bring in coins and place them side by side, the ones which are the oldest and in the finest condition are the ones which are the most valuable. The ones which are old but are in poor condition get some attention from collectors but are not the ones people come to see. However, when an old coin is brought out which is in mint condition, all heads turn and the price is sometimes a thousand fold.

Lives are like coin collections. Some are old. Some are new. Some have been exposed to wear and have faded over time. Others appear to have been protected from the elements and seem to be in mint condition. Some are judged by estimators as valuable. Others are looked over and ruled as only worth face value.

However, there is one major difference between coin collections and mankind. Yes, people may look on our outside and judge us valuable or not valuable based on our outward condition but the

Lord doesn't look at things that way. Yes, people may look at the mint factory from which we came but the Lord doesn't look at things that way. Yes, the world may say that we are young and beautiful or old and cold, but the Lord again does not look at things that way.

According to God's Word as revealed in Holy Scripture, the Lord looks at us through a certain lens. When he pulls our life coin up to his eye, if we have chosen the correct lens, all the Lord sees is perfection. When he gazes at us through the lens that He endorses, all He sees is a proof coin, totally made new, still warm off the press. This lens of course is the precious life, death and resurrection of the Lord Jesus Christ. When the Lord God almighty examines our life coin, if we have chosen His Son, all He sees is righteousness, holiness and perfection. This is only given through Jesus Christ.

I Peter 1:3-7 says it best. "Praise be to the God and Father of our Lord Jesus Christ! In His great mercy he has given us new birth into a living hope through the resurrection of Jesus Christ from the dead, and into an inheritance that can never perish, spoil or fade – kept in heaven for you, who through faith are shielded by God's power…"

Regardless of where we were coined, how old we are or what our outward appearance looks like, we are all seen the same way. We can never perish, spoil or fade. We are kept in a proof condition in the eyes of Heaven because of Jesus Christ.

However, there is the possibility of another viewing from above as well. The other viewing from the Heavenly Father is when He pulls the lens up close and examines a life that shows that there is no Jesus, no resulting sacrifice for sin, no righteousness, no holiness, and no perfection. Why? Because the life coin has chosen to go his own way and never received the free gift of forgiveness from Jesus Christ. I pray that you have chosen the right set of lenses. I pray that your life will be seen from on high through Jesus Christ.

Romans 3:23 says "...for all have sinned and fall short of the glory of God." But when the lens of Jesus examines the life coin Romans 5:8 becomes a reality. "But God demonstrates His love towards us, in that while we were yet sinners, Christ died for us."

At Cointracker.com it says that the 1932 D quarter that I own, if in poor condition, is worth $195. The same quarter in mint, proof, perfect condition is worth $21,000. May all of our lives be seen as in mint perfect condition in the eyes of the only one who really counts.

Scripture reading: Colossians 1:28

Draw near to God and He will draw near to you.

Freezing Rain

On a Thursday evening this past winter an ice storm hit our city. As a result, numerous schools and businesses closed their doors. Even though we hardly ever close, the administrators where I work closed us down as well. Travel was extremely hazardous and leaders did not want individuals to feel that they had to get out into the elements. With this storm's impact not only were the roads and sidewalks dangerous, you also put your safety in harm's way just being outside. Yes, the roads caused cars to go into ditches and in many cases brought traffic to a standstill but the real problem had to do with the trees. Because of the trees, people lost power, roofs on homes were breached and in some areas in times past lives have been taken.

When rain falls from the sky and the temperatures are below freezing, the moisture from the droplets lays down a thin layer of ice on whatever it hits. As this moisture continues to strike the same area, the thickness of the ice sheet grows and grows. Over time, the ice becomes so thick that the sheer weight from the ice begins to impact trees and especially the limbs. If the rain continues throughout the evening then for many trees the weight becomes too great. Eventually, when the weight of the ice exceeds the strength of resistance, the tree branch snaps and falls to the ground. In some cases the entire tree falls to the ground. As you can imagine, whatever is in the way of the tree limb or tree trunk is in harm's way. If a car is underneath it then severe damage is the result. If a roof line is underneath it then a breach in the roof membrane is just around the corner. If a power line is within its reach then electricity is cut to that entire area. And if a person is caught in its path, broken bones or the loss of life is a possibility. This layering of ice occurred on an evening this winter and we felt its impact.

This layering of freezing rain is the culprit. Minute after minute and hour after hour of this accumulating freezing rain eventually causes damage. If this freezing rain were only to last few seconds then there would really be no cause for concern. However, if the temperature stays low and rain repeatedly hits the same mark several hours, then damage is a very real possibility. If such negatives align for a continuous period of time, then there will be consequences.

We are very much like the trees that surround our neighborhoods. During times of sunshine and warmth, we are strong feeling very little against our branches and trunks. Occasionally some rains do come, but they are momentary and actually provide nourishment to our roots. Lightning may even hit our area but only in the rarest of times do they ever directly hit our lives. However, there are instances when we can be repeatedly bombarded by freezing rain. This really does impact our lives. When layers upon layers of difficulty and trial hit our lives, it can be a real challenge. How do we handle such times in our lives? How do we go about the day when such an onslaught of negative circumstances keeps layering away stressing and testing the strength of our limbs?

Every one of us will be exposed to such trials in our lives. Every one of us will feel at one time or another that we are getting pounded by freezing rain. As we know, sunshine as well as freezing rain will fall on all mankind. The goal is not to find ways in which to avoid the freezing rain. The objective is to find the answers on how to get through those days when they do occur. When we finally got out of the house and drove around that night, we saw a humbling sight. There were literally

110

hundreds of trees and limbs which had caved to the pressure. Let's explore very quickly how the maker of the trees, the rain and the temperature would have us approach such times in our lives.

First of all, freezing rain is ok. In fact, we are to welcome it and to consider it a joy to experience. James 1:2-4 talks of this. "My brethren, count it all joy when you fall into various trials, knowing that the testing of your faith produces patience. But let patience have its perfect work, that you may be perfect and complete lacking nothing."

Second, if you are caught in a situation when freezing rain continues to fall on you, then you need to call out for help. Here are three verses which touch on this: I Peter 5:6, 7 "Therefore humble yourselves under the mighty hand of God, that He may exalt you in due time, casting all your care upon Him, for He cares for you." James 5:13 "Is anyone among you suffering? Let him pray." Philippians 4:6, 7 continues with "Be anxious for nothing, but in everything by prayer and supplication, with thanksgiving, let your requests be made known to God; and the peace of God which surpasses all understanding, will guard your hearts and minds in Christ Jesus."

Thirdly, we must know that somehow and in some way God is going to work out the situation for good. Romans 8:28 speaks of this. "And we know that all things work together for good to those who love God, to those who are the called according to His purpose."

Lastly, that the Lord is not going to allow us to be in situations that we and the Lord cannot handle together. I Corinthians 1:13 says "No temptation (trial) has overtaken you except such as is common to man; but God is faithful, who will not allow you to be tempted beyond what you are able, but with the temptation will also make the way of escape, that you may be able to bear it."

Freezing rain is going to fall into our lives. Many of us may succumb to the trial in many ways. Branches may snap or entire trees may topple as we retreat into unbelief, or various coping mechanisms used to dull the reality of the situation in which we are exposed. Some of us may fight it with busyness and preoccupation with careers, hobbies or countless other distractions but none of these will bring lasting peace and true perspective. None will bring true comfort like the comfort that the Lord promises.

II Corinthians says it best. "Blessed be the God and Father of our Lord Jesus Christ, the Father of mercies and God of all comfort, who comforts us in all our tribulation that we may be able to comfort those who are in any trouble, with the comfort with which we ourselves are comforted by God."

Jesus provides shelter from the freezing rain. Jesus provides comfort from the pain of the circumstances. Jesus provides rest. Jesus promises this in Matthew 11:28-30. "Come to Me, all you who labor and are heavy laden, and I will give you rest. Take my yoke (a burden shared together) upon you and learn from Me, for I am gentle and lowly in heart, and you will find rest for your souls. For My yoke is easy and My burden is light."

It is cold outside and it looks like rain. Get ready. Be strong.

Scripture reading: I Peter 5:6-7

Draw near to God and He will draw near to you.

Hot and Cold

The weather has been crazy here in North Carolina this this year. One Tuesday several weeks back it was 75 degrees. People by the droves were out for walks, riding bikes and working in yards. Two days later on Thursday it was 25 degrees. Windows were frosted over and ice was forming on mud puddles, ponds and lakes. These extreme temperatures set us up for high winds as well. Some wind gauges recorded winds gusting close to 60 miles per hour on Thursday taking down numerous trees and knocking out power to many neighborhoods. 75 degrees on one day and 25 degrees just two days later was amazing to experience.

Even though it was a challenge to constantly make adjustments to our thermostats, choosing the right clothing for these extremes of hot and cold was fairly easy. When it was hot, we all knew exactly what to wear. Most of us put on a short sleeved t-shirt and broke out the summer shorts. When it was 25 degrees outside, though not wanting to revisit winter again, the choice was easy as well. I pulled out a long-sleeved shirt, a sweater, a sports jacket and covered it all with my navy pea coat. When it was hot we knew how to dress and when it was cold we knew what to put on as well. The trouble came on the in-between day. The difficulty came when the day was neither hot nor cold but a mixture.

On Wednesday, the temperature would not make up its mind. It was warm at first and then cold in the mid afternoon. Warmth greeted us in the morning only to change directions later on in the day. Many of us thought that dressing light was a good decision only to adjust our wardrobe when those chilling winds came through later on that day. These fluctuations were very confusing. I thought that sunglasses and light clothing would rule the day only to have my winter outerwear take priority. The weather would not make up its mind. When it was hot I was ready for it. When it was cold I was ready as well. But when the weather was neither hot nor cold, but lukewarm and inconsistent, it is hard to judge and to dress accordingly.

So it is in our walk with the Lord. It is easy to notice in our lives when we are hot and when we are cold spiritually. When we are hot, we cannot wait to read his word, fellowship with other believers and encourage buddies to do the same. When cold we can see it as well. Our thoughts are oftentimes far from Him, we seldom think of His love for us and we hardly ever want to pray to Him or listen to His word. Those are times that we can confront fairly easily. If hot, we know we are to thank Him and continue with His word in our hearts and minds and when we are cold we know that we need to turn around and get going in the direction toward Him. The hard part is when we are neither hot nor cold but lukewarm. Like this past Wednesday when the weather would not make up its mind, we too oftentimes do not make up our mind. We too, are all over the place. We start out hot only to fluctuate to cold. As you can imagine, this is not what a steady and faithful walk with our Lord should look like. I have been there and maybe this day some of you may be struggling with the same thing.

Why is this so in our lives? Why do we allow such vacillations to happen in our walks with the Lord? Though every case is a little different because of life experiences and circumstances, I do believe that there is one possibility which sets us up for such variations when we should be standing fast. I believe that it is a lack of spiritual wisdom and courageous application of our Lord's inspired guidelines to life. We struggle with consistency because we repeatedly are succumbing to the cultural and contemporary philosophies of the modern times. His word and His thoughts are not bathing our minds, something else is. Ephesians 4:14 warns us of this. "…that we should no longer be children, tossed to and fro and carried about with every wind of doctrine, by the trickery of men, in the cunning craftiness of deceitful plotting…"

Colossians 2:8 confronts this tendency to follow popular culture and individual philosophies as well. "Beware lest anyone cheat you through philosophy and empty deceit, according to the tradition of men, according to the basic principles of the world, and not according to Christ."

You see, I think that we are tossed to and fro and are cheated by the worlds' thinking because we are not storing up and applying spiritual knowledge. II Timothy 4:3-5 continues with this thought by stating, "For the time will come when they will not endure sound doctrine, but according to their own desires, because they have itching ears, they will heap up for themselves teachers, and they will turn their ears away from the truth, and be turned aside to fables. But you be watchful in all things…"

Resist the temptation to always go counter to the loving instructions from our Lord. Fight the inclination to join an individual's opinion or personal philosophy and not the words of the One who knows you best and loves you most. Stand strong and courageous in the face of what majority opinion is trending. Jesus Christ did live. Jesus did walk on water. Jesus did heal a man born blind and made the lame to walk. Jesus did rise from the dead. Jesus is God and His words are truth. It is difficult to stand solo sometimes when your friends say that following the God of this universe is antiquated. However, just know this, God is pleased when you do and He is proud of you standing with Him and for Him.

When it is hot, dress appropriately. When it is cold, dress warm. When life is coming at you being both hot and cold wanting you to be lukewarm in your walk with the Lord, stay strong and faithful and your reward will be great. He is the way, the truth and the life. In His presence we can truly find the answers to life's most difficult questions. Stay the course.

Scripture reading: II Corinthians 10:5, Romans 12:1, 2

As always, draw near to God and He will draw near to you.

The Baton

I am pumped. In just a couple days our university is going to be hosting the first track meet of the year. Teams from all across the region will descend upon our city aiming to record their personal records. Teams and individual competitors will be giving all that they have in hopes of placing or possibly winning their event. Pole-vaulters, high jumpers and long jumpers will be straining for every centimeter in height or distance. Discus and hammer throwers as well as shot putters will be hoping that their divot will be the one farthest out. And then those on the track, with their shoes squarely in the starting blocks, will be striving to either get out fast and to finish strong. Every event will show evidence of their God-given ability, their winter conditioning and their work on the exchanges.

What exchanges am I talking about, you may be asking? As one who has ran on track and field teams beginning in elementary school, the exchanges that I am talking about only happen in relay races. These exchanges involve a small hollow aluminum stick about one foot in length called a baton. The baton is the primary focus of the relay race. The goal of the relay is for the runners to get the baton across the finish line. There are four members of every relay race and each member must run with the baton aiming to make a clean exchange to the next runner until the last runner crosses the finish line. Whether the exchanges are blind exchanges like the four by 100 meter relay or open exchanges like the four by 400 relay, they all are critical as to whether the team finishes their best.

Individual relay team members work on this exchange everyday at practice. The first runner has to make sure that he gets the baton to the next runner so he or she can show their skills. Each runner has a job to do and one of these jobs is to get the baton to the next person. If the baton is dropped, then the next person assigned to contribute is not given a chance. If the exchange is not made then the potential, the energy and the impact of the next athlete giving his or her best is never seen or felt. The baton must be handed off at just the right time, in just the right manner, with eyes open, hands open and with feet ready to hit the track surface.

A spiritual baton is in your hand. It is up to you to hand it off to the next person in line. Without you handing it off, the next person on your team will not be able to reach his fullest potential. You have been entrusted with much. Now it is your turn to give it away. You cannot run the race of life holding onto this wonderful gift that you have in your hands. God's word clarifies what this baton is. God's word describes the job that you and I need to do.

"And Jesus came and spoke to them saying, "All authority has been given to Me in heaven and on earth. Go therefore and make disciples of all the nations, baptizing them in the name of the Father and of the Son and of the Holy Spirit, teaching them to observe all things that I have commanded you, and lo, I am with you always, even to the end of the age. Amen."

The baton that you have in your hands is the good news of Jesus Christ. We cannot run around the track and hold onto it. We have to give it away. Are you passing on your baton? Are you looking for individuals in your life who you can hand it off to? Or, are you sitting on the good news just enjoying the blessings of our God by yourself? We are always supposed to be ready. We are always to be looking for someone to hand it off to.

I Peter 3:15 says "But sanctify the Lord God in your hearts, and always be ready to give a defense to everyone who asks you a reason for the hope that is in you, with meekness and fear,.."

Are you ready? Do you care for the souls of your friends, your family members and those who cross your paths each day? If we do not care, who will? If we do not share the baton, the good news with them, who will? When you do share it, the Lord describes us in a certain way. When we share he says that our feet are beautiful.

Romans 10:14, 15 "How then shall they call on Him in whom they have not believed? And how shall they believe in Him of whom they have not heard? And how shall they hear without a preacher? And how shall they preach unless they are sent? As it is written: How beautiful are the feet of those who preach the gospel of peace, who bring glad tidings of good things!"

Finally, for those who run track there is an indoor season and outdoor season. After indoors and outdoors there are the summer months which are historically the off season. Regardless of the time of year, track athletes who want to do well will continue to run. They will never hang up their shoes. Likewise, as runners carrying the most precious gift ever known to mankind, may we never hang up our shoes.

As the apostle Paul told young leader in I Timothy 4: 2 "Preach the Word, be prepared in season and out of season; correct, rebuke and encourage with great patience and careful instruction."

As we all pursue the tasks set before us each day, may we never forget that we are our Lord's representatives. May we never forget that we are His ambassadors. May we never forget that we are now His mouthpieces delivering the good news to a lost and hurting world. You have the baton. You have the good news. Share it often. Pass it on. You can do it. We can do it.

Scripture reading: Proverbs 11:30

As always, draw near to God and He will draw near to you.

Putting Off to Put On

After numerous trips to fabric stores with my wife looking at dozens and dozens of patterns, we finally picked out a pattern that goes best on our dining room chairs. After closely examining our wall colors, our area rug pattern and our furniture, we chose a brand new look for the seats at the dining room table. With some needle nose pliers in hand along with a couple screwdrivers and a staple gun, my wife and I went to work yesterday afternoon on our much anticipated chair project.

With a roll of the new upholstery on site and a new look eagerly awaiting us, we still had a big decision to make. Should we just cover over the old seat covering or should we start new? Rather than take off the hundreds of staples and the well-worn seat coverings, we had to decide if we were to just cover over the old with the new? However, as we thought about this approach, we realized that the old stains and marks would still be there. We thought about how the old blemishes might in fact show through the new upholstery. The new would be on the outside but it would not be a completely new on the inside. The old would still be there. It would not be completely be made new. In fact, we would be hanging onto the old.

We decided that we would not put the new on top of the old. We decided that we would take the time necessary and remove the old marked and stained upholstery that needed to be replaced. Though our hands were sore and marked with some blisters, the old staples were plucked and the old covering was removed. In its place we installed brand new perfectly fitted upholstery. My wife and I backed away from the nine chairs that were redone and smiled. If was a lot of work but we now have a completely new look. The old is not just covered over. It is brand new. We put off the old so that we could put on the new.

In our lives, much like this chair project, we have a similar choice to make. Once we hear of the new life provided in Jesus Christ, we too have a decision to make. Much like the new upholstery, we too can attempt to just staple over the old with the new. However, the old will never have really gone away. The old mindset, old priorities, old habits, and old worldview will still remain. In order for our lives to be made completely new there needs to be a putting off of the old. In order for Jesus Christ to truly make our lives new from the inside out there must be a tearing away, a turning away, a putting off of the old. We must be willing to turn from our old life, die to that old self and put on the new self, the new life in Christ Jesus. Without this putting off, our old life will always be just under the surface much like a chair's old upholstery just being covered over with new.

Gods words of life says this best in Ephesians 4:21-24 "...if indeed you have heard Him and have been taught by Him, as the truth is in Jesus: that you put off, concerning your former conduct, the old man which grows corrupt according to deceitful lusts, and be renewed in the spirit of your mind, and that you put on the new man which was created according to God, in true righteousness and holiness."

Our loving, kind, merciful and gracious Lord wants all mankind to come to Him and to be made new. 2 Peter talks of this in 3:9. "The Lord is not slack concerning His promise, as some count slackness, but is longsuffering towards us, not willing that any should perish but that all should come to repentance."

He does not desire for one human being to perish but for all of us to turn around. This is repentance. He wants us all to turn around. He wants us to put off the old self. He wants us to rip out the staples and take on this new life, this new creation that is available in Jesus. "Therefore, if anyone is in Christ, he is a new creation, old things have passed away; behold, all things have become new."

There is an old covering that we all must deal with. The bible says that all have sinned and fall short of the glory of God. (Romans 3:23) And the penalty for having this sin, this old life covering is separation from God or what the bible calls death. The only way for this sin to be put off is by believing that Jesus Christ is God in the flesh, that He came, that He lived, died for our sins and was raised on the third day. When we believe God, we are in essence putting our trust in Him. When we believe that Jesus is alive having conquered death, He rips off the old covering, the old sin filled life and gives us a new one.

Will we still sin in our lives? Yes. But it will not be our nature. Our new nature is what is there now. The old nature is ripped off and when we sin, we need to confess it, admit that it is not my new life and move on, walking in newness of life.

So my challenge to you all this day is this: Are you living like one who has had his life been made new? Or, are you living in such a way that the old covering is still being your master? Put off the old life, turn from the old and walk in the newness of life. Put on the new self and walk daily with Him. If He is in your life, He will never leave you nor forsake you. If He is in your life, you have what you need to live life with power, with purpose, with peace and totally pardoned ripped clean of the sin which used to cover and fill your life.

Stay the course. Keep the faith. Speak to Him throughout the day. He is your biggest fan, your strength and your pathway to a life of meaning and eternal impact.

Scripture reading: Colossians 3:5-10

Draw near to God and He will draw near to you.

Only One Person for the Job

Over 140 individuals have applied for a position that we have open in our office. Last week we conducted 12 phone interviews and this week we are scheduled to perform five Skype interviews. Eventually we will bring at least two people to campus and from those two we will select one. We will select only one because there is only one person for that job. Only one person will have the duties that we have carved out for him or her to execute. Only one person will oversee those under his or her care. Only one person will supervise, monitor and schedule the facilities, the budgets, the programs and the marketing efforts assigned to them. We have a job that we need to have done and only one person can do it.

In this exciting process, we have been looking for the exact skill set which will meet our campus needs. We are looking for one with the education, with the experiences and with the desire to make the position everything that it can possibly be. Filling this position with the right person is critical to our success. With a new sports field coming on line this summer and a new indoor gymnasium renovation project on the horizon, we need an individual on board who not only has what it takes to maintain our programs but one who can catapult us forward. There is only one person for this job and if we do not fill it, then the work will not get done. If we do not find the right person for this job, with the right abilities, talents and passion level, then we will not be the department that we are capable of becoming. There is an important job to be done and we desperately need the right person in place to make sure that our needs are addressed. Our office needs this person, our students deserve this person and our entire campus community expects this person to be in place soon. If it doesn't happen soon, then many will be missing out.

Do you know that you are the one person for a job? Do you know that there is a position created for you that desperately needs your skill set? Do you know that there is a task which fits you perfectly? Do you know that without your attention to this job that it will not get done? Do you know that there is a calling that you were in fact born to perform? Yes, there is a job that if not filled by you, this community, this city and this world would be less than it could possibly be.

Do you know who posted the job description and put your name on it? Do you know who knows and has qualified you to perform it? Do you know that there is One who will have your back, will give you the support and will be giving you the strength to get it done? The One who wrote the job title and description with your name in mind is your Creator. The One who has a job for you that no one else can do is your Almighty God. The One who is banking on you to be His hands and His feet in this endeavor is the One who knows you best and who knows that you have what it takes to do this thing set before you.

Ephesians 2:10 says "For we are His workmanship, created in Christ Jesus for good works, which God prepared beforehand that we should walk in them."

You have a job to do which is from the Lord. He will equip you. He will guide you. He will show you the way. He will be with you every step of the way. The big question is this: Are you willing to listen to His call and respond to what He would have you do? Fulfillment, peace, purpose and impact are waiting for you when you say yes to his job offer. It is a choice isn't it? Though examples are numerous, there is one other job option which will cry out for our attention our entire life. It is this, I want to do it 'my way'. Yes, there is His way which is an unbelievable adventure with the Almighty God of creation and then there is our own way, limited in reach, limited in impact and limited in the blessings from on high. Choose wisely this day. I urge you to read our Lord's job description and accept the offer.

In the Old Testament, Joshua and God's people stood at a crossroads. Joshua knew that there would be many enticements set before them all in life. He would encourage them to choose the Lord but in the end, he could only say what he was going to do. In Joshua 24:15 he writes, "And if it seems evil to you to serve the Lord, choose for yourselves this day whom you will serve, whether the gods which your fathers served that were on the other side of the River; or the gods of the Amorites, in whose land you dwell. But as for me, and my house, we will serve the Lord."

Who will you serve this day? Who are you going to serve with your life? Have you considered serving the One who has written a job description that fits your life perfectly? He has a job for you, a calling for you, a place in this world where you will find meaning, joy and impact. Seek Him this day. Draw close to the words on the job description and accept the offer. If you do sign on the dotted line, I promise you that you will not only find your true place, that all of heaven will be on your side. And then some day, you will stand before your Maker and you will hear the words that will ring in your ears throughout all eternity. Those words will be "Well done, good and faithful servant."

Life is not over. We all have some work to do. Find yours. Find the thing that our Lord would have you do. We need you. The world needs you. The church body needs you. Ephesians says it best. "… from whom the whole body, joined and knit together by what every joint supplies, according to the effective working by which every part does its share, causes growth of the body for edifying of itself in love."

Scripture reading: Ephesians 4:16

Draw close to God and He will draw close to you.

Spiritual Fitness

I went for a jog this morning. My wife Debbie and our dog Sadie went down to the Greenway where the terrain is flat. I ran for 17 minutes and walked for another 15 minutes. It was a good start back for I had not been able to run for at least 3 weeks. I was out of breath right out of the gate and labored the entire run but got it done. It was amazing how out of shape I felt. After this morning, it is hard to imagine that I have run several 5K's, a half marathon and a full marathon as well (26.2 miles). Now, I am out of shape. How did could I have let this happen?

After thinking on my current fitness level, a few things have come to mind as to the reasons for this backslide. First of all, I just got busy with other things. Second, I did not pre-decide each day the time and location that I was going to work out. Third, I did not have a goal, like a race in front of me, pushing me to stay on a plan. Fourth, I did not have anyone going running with me. I did not have anyone to keep me accountable. Finally, I was not fully convinced that working out was that good for me, my family and the example that I set before others.

This can happen in our walks with the Lord as well. In only a short time, we can be like me and only look back at what I used to be able to do and the walk that I used to have with the Lord. In only a short period of time, without deciding beforehand that I need to set time aside for the Lord, I can get busy, get distracted and neglect or forget a daily divine appointment with my Heavenly Father. In only a short time, without knowing, I can forget about the goal of being like Christ in everything I say, think or do. In only a short time, I can forget about my brothers who can go along with me on this race to know, honor and serve the Lord who gave Himself for me. In only a short time, I can forget about the spiritual strength I need for myself, my family and a watching world.

One day without walking closely with the Lord can turn into two days, then three, then a week, then two weeks and a month. Then, you will get on the track like I did this morning and say to yourself, "Wow, I am so out of shape." Spiritually the words may be, "Wow, I am far from the Lord right now. I have drifted far from the One who I need to be next to every single moment of every day."

Stay close to Him each and every day. Build your spiritual muscles, your spiritual wind, your spiritual endurance and your spiritual walk. Build it one strand at a time. If you do your rope of spiritual fitness will end in a close walk with the Lord. It then will be so strong that it will handle the tests of life.

Here are some scriptures to remind us of our need to come to Him daily. Don't get out of shape. Stay ready to run a 10K at any time, in any place.

Scripture readings: Acts 17:11 "Examined the scriptures every day…"

2 Corinthians 4:16 "…we are being renewed day by day.."

Psalm 5:3 "In the morning, O Lord, you hear my voice,."

Draw near to God and He will draw near to you

My Truck

I have a 1997 Toyota T-100 truck which I drive to work every day. I have used this truck for just about everything under the sun. I have filled it up with mulch, with bags of rock, with bags of concrete and even filled it to the top with 300 degree asphalt which I needed to fix holes in the front of our property. This red truck has hauled furniture, sports equipment and even a half a dozen baseball players when they needed rides. It has seen much over the years, now topping 180,000 miles this past month. The interior is starting to show much wear and the paint is starting to fade quite a bit. Why would anyone keep an old truck like this around for so long? Why should I deal with the squeaks, the dents and of course the comments and stares from friends? Why do I keep it? Why do I hang onto this old truck?

I keep this truck because of all of the memories that it represents. I keep this truck because it connects the years of my life. You see this truck was there when my youngest son was just born, my oldest daughter played soccer, my youngest daughter went off to ballet and my oldest son started Little League. This truck is not only functional, it is a reminder of days gone by. When I crank up this old red truck every morning, I am connecting its start to the starts that it has given me for well over 100,000 miles. You see, if I were to trade out and get new, I would lose a little bit. I would lose a little of where I have come from. You see when I put my truck in motion, I am going with an old friend, big red, red thunder, rojo rider. What does my red truck have to do with my Christian life? What does the memories which come with a piece of steel have to do with my walk with Christ? The point that I want to make is this: don't be in a hurry to cast away the things of old for something new. I know that new technology is exciting. I know that new endeavors are fun and new relationships can be intriguing but remember newer is not always better. The Lord said that He is the same yesterday, today and forever. The Lord does not change. He is the consistent part of my life which I can depend on each and every day. Though He is eternal, every morning He is with me. Though He is omnipotent, every morning He is there for me. He has been there for me from the time that I first met Him until today. Just because you have known the Lord for some time now, don't be in a hurry to make a trade and invest in something else. Cherish His timeless thoughts, His ageless perspective and His eternal will for your life.

Spend time with Him, speak with Him, make memories together and build connections to the abundant life He desires for you. Get comfortable with the Lord and His presence as I am comfortable in my old red truck. My truck is just metal which does not satisfy. The Lord is life and will give you a life that is full and meaningful.

Scripture reading: Psalm 139 "O Lord, you have searched me and you know me. You know when I ..."

Draw near to God and He will draw near to you.

Birthdays

My mom turned 80 years old a couple days ago. Since she lives on Kodiak Island in Alaska, we decided to contact a local florist for a nice bouquet of flowers to be delivered to her on her birthday. When I called wishing her a happy birthday, she had received the gift and had already cleared the front table putting the flowers in the middle of the dining room table for her and dad to see. You could tell that she really appreciated the gesture.

Modern technology helped with mom's birthday as well. My younger brother posted a 'Happy Birthday' wish on Facebook and within seconds word got out in the small town of Kodiak. Mom and dad were at the local high school gymnasium watching the girls varsity basketball team play when one of my brother's friends decided to add to the fun. After reading the post on his phone, he looked across the gym and saw my mom and dad watching the game. Since my brother was not there to do it, this fine young man, during a break in the action walked across the gym, went into the stands and gave my mother a big hug wishing her a happy birthday. He told her, "Mrs. Floyd, I know your youngest son could not be here to give you this hug, so I thought that I would do it for him. Happy birthday."

A birthday is a special thing. It is a unique celebration of a magical event which comes only once a year. It is a time when those encircling the one having the birthday can say the things that need to be said. Gifts and cards are often given informing the birthday boy or girl of his or her importance. One on one statements are many times shared vocally in these cards or gifts as well. Phrases like the following are commonplace: "I love you bud." "Thank you for all that you do and mean to me." "I am so glad that you are in my life." "You are such wonderful person." "You light up our lives." And then my favorite which gets to the core of the day, "Happy birthday, the world is a better place because you are in it. I am so glad that you were born." If you are reading this sentence, you have a birthday as well. You also have a special day that brings celebration. You have a unique day as well. It is the day of your birth. It is the day when you were physically brought into this world. Our physical birthdays are wonderful and I enjoy celebrating with those I know and love.

There is another birthday that is wonderful as well. In fact, it surpasses the first. For me, this second birthday blows past the importance of my birthday May 1st birthday. There is a birthday, which like our first birthday, marks the start of life. It is the date of our second birthday. All of mankind has the first birthday. Not all of mankind has a second birthday. The story of the necessity of this second birth was told by Jesus over 2000 years ago. A man came to Jesus and asked him a foundational question. Jesus, in his reply, announced the opportunity for all of mankind to have a second birthday.

John 3:1-8 "Now there was a man of the Pharisees named Nicodemus, a member of the Jewish ruling council. He came to Jesus at night and said, "Rabbi, we know you are a teacher who has come from God. For no one could perform the miraculous signs you are doing if God were not with him." In reply Jesus declared, "I tell you the truth, no one can see the kingdom of God unless he is born again." ...vs 7. You should not be surprised at my saying, You must be born again."

My first birthday is May 1st. Though not totally positive of the exact day, my second birthday is in early November. You see in early November of 1979, in my dorm room, at my study desk, on the fourth floor of Palo Verde West, on the campus of Arizona State University, I repented of my sins and received Jesus Christ as the Lord and Savior of my life. I said something like this. "Dear Lord, I believe that Jesus Christ is the Son of God, and that He died on the cross, was buried, and rose again that I might have forgiveness of my sins and can experience His indwelling presence in my life. I have this day received Him and do confess that Jesus Christ is my Lord and Savior. Amen." At that very moment I had a spiritual second birth. There were no fireworks, no band playing and no blue cigars. There is one thing that did happen at that moment. I became a child of God. John 1:12 confirms this when it states: "Yet to all who received him, to those who believed in his name, he gave the right to become children of God."

I know that you have your first birthday and I cannot wait to hear of the date. However, I do want to ask you another question. Do you have a second birthday? If not, like me all those years ago, you can have one as well. In fact, you can do it in the quiet of the room or office which you are right now. Your first birthday got you here. Your second one will take you much further. Your second birth, a spiritual birth, will make you a child of God, give you every spiritual blessing possible and will secure you a place in heaven. In heaven, you will be alongside all of us who have a second birthday as well, for all of eternity. Happy birthday.

Scripture reading: I John 5:12 "He who has the Son..., Romans 3:23, Romans 6:23, Romans 10:9

Draw near to God and He will draw near to you.

Generation iY

The generation which was born after 1990 is called the iY Generation. The i stands for i-phone, i-pad, i-pod, i-everything. All this generation has ever known has been the latest and greatest in technology. A group of students were recently quoted in a survey stating that technology to them is equal to air and water. Technology is no longer a tool but a needed appendage says Tim Elmore author of the book "Generation iY". In fact, a study out of Villanova University has revealed that there are now cases where young people have been found not sleep walking but sleep texting. One group of students said that they bring their phones into the shower with them. They put the phone in a plastic bag and shower with it close at hand so not to miss any new post or text. Studies have confirmed that many in this generation sleep with their phones next to them, turned on. Because of this night time connection, research is now showing a large percentage of 16-24 year olds are away from technology for only one hour per day. Why do our young people always have to be available? Why does this next generation of leaders never want to miss anything? Why is this generation so attached to their technology pieces?

Let me ask you something as we head into this day and approaching weekend. What would our lives be like if we were so interested in being available, so interested in being connected and so interested in hearing from,.... our Heavenly Father? What if we went to bed with thoughts of His presence in our lives? What if we rose up with His words echoing in our minds? What if we were so close to our loving Heavenly Father that we would describe Him as an appendage? What if we put Jesus on the level of water and air? If we did, we would know our Maker. We

136

would then walk with Him. We would know His will for our lives. He would be our strength. We would depend on Him and nothing else.

Lets walk with Jesus in this way. When we reach for our cell phone, when we long to see the next post, when we cannot function without reading the last text, let's think about what our world would be like if our thoughts were of Christ in that way? Reach for Jesus. He will satisfy. He is the connection that we all so desperately need.

Scripture reading: Matthew 6:33, Colossians 3:1-2

Draw near to God and He will draw near to you.

Making a Withdrawal

I went by the bank a couple days back. I needed to get some money for a haircut. I pulled into the bank parking lot and walked over to the ATM from which I normally get cash. As I walked over to the bank's ATM, I was very confident. I was confident that I would be able to get some money. I was confident that when I put my card into the machine that it would kick out the needed cash that I wanted. You see I was confident that I was going to get some money because several days before, really for several months beforehand, I had been making deposits into that same account. I was confident because I had been depositing into the account consistently pay period by pay period. I knew that I had the money.

As I approached the machine, I pulled out my wallet, found my card and put it into the machine. I punched in my access code, keyed in the amount that I needed and presto, out came a crisp 20 dollar bill. My bank account had the needed money in it. It was not empty. I grabbed the 20 dollars, took the receipt and went about my business. I was able to make a withdrawal because I had been faithful in putting money in for days, weeks and years prior to the time that I needed it. I know from experience that if I were to try to withdraw money and had not been depositing any monies earlier, I would not have gotten any money out. You get out what you put in.

What is the status of your spiritual bank account? Have you been regularly, consistently, day by day making deposits into your relationship with the Lord Almighty? Have you been investing into the relationship by a steady flow of Bible Study? Have you been laying up treasures in heaven by engaging in prayer in every situation possible? Have you been making deposits into your spiritual bank account by talking of Him often, thinking about His will repeatedly, and pondering how to know Him better?

There will come a time in your life when you will need to draw upon God's resources. There will come a time when you will need to ask of the Lord what only He can supply. There will come a time in your life when you will need to use your card and you will need some help. Start investing today. Start depositing today. Start sowing into your walk with the Lord today. Every one of us needs the Lord. When the bank account of a close and intimate relationship with the Lord has been invested in, your faith in His decisions and provision will be strengthened more and more. What is the status of your bank account? Check the balance this evening and if it needs some cash deposits don't wait. Go for a walk and speak with Him; open up the Holy Scriptures or maybe even wrestle on a verse of scripture with a friend. When you do, the balance in your spiritual bank account will begin to grow.

Philippians 4:6, 7 says "Do not be anxious about anything, but in everything, by prayer and petition, with thanksgiving, present your requests to God. And the peace of God which transcends all understanding will guard your hearts and your minds in Christ Jesus."

Galatians 5:22 "But the fruit of the Spirit (a life indwelt and walking with the Lord) is love, joy, peace, patience, kindness, goodness, faithfulness, gentleness and self-control."

I will be looking forward to seeing you all at the ATM this week. My intentions are to make some deposits as well. May you all have lots of deposit slips tucked you're your life as you stop by the local ATM each and every day.

Scripture reading: John 15:5

Draw near to God and He will draw near to you.

In the Beloved

When an individual places his faith and trust in Jesus Christ, he is forgiven, given eternal life, and has received every spiritual blessing available. However, there is one other thing which happens when one comes to Christ. We are accepted. We are accepted into the family of God. The Bible says that we are accepted, that we are in the Beloved.

In Ephesians 1:6 it says this,"...to the praise of the glory of His grace, by which He made us accepted in the Beloved." What does this 'accepted in the Beloved' mean? It means that because we are identified with Him by faith, that His goodness is now also our goodness. Because our Savior and Lord is the Beloved of the Father and possesses all the goodness of the Father, we also are the beloved of the Father and possess all His goodness. We are accepted in the Beloved.

In the fall of 1980, I trusted Jesus Christ as my savior and my Lord while I was a freshman at Arizona State University. A man by the name of Gary Pageant faithfully met with me on a weekly basis walking me through the truths of scripture and particularly the call of Jesus Christ. One day as Gary was talking with me, he told me that I should start thinking about attending a local church. I took him up on the offer and attended a church on McClintock Drive in Tempe. After a very challenging and encouraging service, I found myself hanging out in the lobby waiting for my ride back to campus. While I was standing there, a married couple and their two children came up to me and introduced themselves. Their names were Don and Ann Craw. They asked me if I would like to be treated to some lunch. Being an always hungry college student, myself along with another freshman from ASU went over to their house for lunch. It was a wonderful meal. The next Sunday came around and I decided to go back to the same church. When I was in the lobby, Mr. and Mrs. Craw approached me again. This time they introduced me to some other folks in the church. As my friend and I we were starting to head back to campus, they asked us if we would like some lunch again. We went home with them again enjoying another splendid lunch. Week after week I continued to attend this local church and many times the Craws invited me home for lunch.

Christmas break finally arrived and I could not wait to fly home to Kodiak, Alaska. After the very welcomed three week break, I flew back to Tempe landing at the International Airport. Once having landed, I had a couple options of getting back to the main campus. However, in order to save some money, I decided to call someone for a ride. The Craws were the only family I knew so I called them. Within minutes they were at the airport. As we started to drive to campus Mr. Craw said, "Max since it is kind of late would you like to spend the night with us tonight? We can get you over to campus first thing tomorrow morning." I said that it sounded great.

Once we got to their home I told them that any couch or area on the floor would be fine. They would not have it. Mr. Craw said, "Ann, please get the special guest room ready." He turned to me and said, "Max we have a special room that we reserve for our family and special guests. We would like you to stay there." Kind of stunned, I said alright and followed them to a large, comfortable room, just off the main den area. A few minutes later, after I got settled in, Mrs. Craw called me up to the kitchen. Opening up the refrigerator Mrs. Craw said "Max, you help yourself to whatever that is in here. There is lots of lunch meat here, snacks in the pantry and soft drinks in the garage. You take whatever you like." Heading back downstairs I thought to myself. "Wow, I have known this family only a couple months and they have given me lunches, given me their best room and now have given me free rein of their kitchen." In the morning something else happened that I will never forget.

As we got ready to drive to campus, Mr. Craw pointed to something as we were backing out of the driveway. He said, "Max, see that truck over there. If you ever need a vehicle to drive, you just call us and you can use it for as long as you like." Continual lunches, their best room, free rein of the kitchen and now their truck. I did not know what to say.

What was going on? I did not know then but I do know now. You see I was accepted in the Beloved. I was family. I was a brother. I was kin. I was accepted. After watching my walk and desire to grow in Christ, whatever privilege the Craws family had, I now had the same privileges. I was a Christian who had needs and they did what they could to meet them. These dear friends have both passed away and are with the Lord now. I cannot wait to see them again someday. I will thank them again for the way that they accepted me just as Jesus Christ accepted me when I put my trust in Him.

When we trust Jesus, we are not only at peace with God, have our sins forgiven, and receiving life everlasting along with other spiritual blessings, we also receive one other thing. We are accepted. We are accepted and are in the Beloved. We are now a child of God joined together with all of those who also have come to know Jesus Christ.

In Christ, you are not alone. You are never by yourself. The Lord is always there, always available, always able to meet you and comfort you. In addition to this however, you are also accepted and in the Beloved. Know that the Band of Brothers and fellow sisters in Christ are on your side. Know that fellow Christians at work are on your side. Know that relatives who have trusted in Christ are on your side. Know that your friends in Christ everywhere are on your side. Why? Because you are accepted and are in the Beloved.

Scripture reading: I John 3:1, I Peter 2:9-10, John 1:12

Draw near to God and He will draw near to you.

White as Snow

One Saturday this past winter, I woke up to snowfall. I went to my window and looked outside and saw a soft, quiet, steady, blanket of snow gently falling from a light gray sky. It was very peaceful and serene. Though none of it was sticking because of the warm day the day before, I still watched intently being mesmerized by the change of pace which snow always delivers. Instead of rushing around getting to the chores of the day, I stopped, looked outside and bathed in the beauty of creation's splendor.

Even though I was born and raised on Kodiak Island in Alaska and have seen my share of snowfall, each time it appears it still creates in me a sense of wonder. To this day I still stop in my tracks and pause, though sometimes only momentarily, to think of things in life. I think of the current scene with the picture of white everywhere. I also think of the upcoming future decisions contemplating whether businesses and schools will be delayed. Most of the time however, I think of past days. My mind drifts happily back to snow forts in the front yard, snowball fights between neighboring families and of course the hill down the road where everyone went sledding. Great times were interestingly re-lived again that morning just by waking up and being greeted by a picture of snow.

Snow has meaning in life as well. Snow not only denotes winter, cold and slippery slopes, snow also denotes purity, cleanness, and starting anew. As you begin this weekend, ponder the truth of what Jesus Christ did for you, for me and for all of those who believe in him. As you begin your list of chores, your list of tasks and your study plans, contemplate for a moment the cleansing which Jesus did for you at the cross. Ponder afresh today how God Almighty sent His Son to wash away your sins making your life as white as snow. Think just for a moment, this moment, about the great gift that Jesus has given and the opportunity to walk in newness of life, because of His great love for us. Romans 5:8 says "But God demonstrates His love for us in that while we were yet sinners, Christ died for us."

I enjoyed the snow that Saturday morning a while back. But more than that, because of sin being washed whiter than snow there is an opportunity to enjoy each day, forgiven life totally new. This we receive when we turn from our selfish ways and turn to the one who cleanses, the one who forgives, the one who declares us clean. This is available to those who puts their trust in Him. One of my favorite verses in the Bible tells the story of the privilege we truly have in Jesus. Isaiah 1:18 "Come now, and let us reason together," says the Lord, "though your sins are like scarlet, they shall be as white as snow; though they are red like crimson, they shall be as wool."

Have a great day as you enjoy the blessings of being one whose sins are as white as snow. Go and walk worthy of the calling that you, that I, have received. Walk worthy, walk humbly, walk appreciatively, walk in wonder as you remember the whiter than snow life which portrays your position before God.

May your day by day experience match your position before our most kind, most loving, most merciful Heavenly Father.

What a privilege to be fellow recipients of this gracious blanket of snow.

Scripture reading: II Corinthians 5:17

Draw near to God and He will draw near to you.

Pre-Emergent

I went to the Home Depot a couple weeks back after church with the intent of finding something which is critical to apply to lawns this time of year. Every late February until the middle of March, every home owner who wants to have a nice lawn must put down pre-emergent. Pre-emergent is a unique mixture of a special herbicide and the traditional fertilizers such as nitrogen, phosphorus and potassium. This pre-emergent needs to go onto your lawn at just the right time. Traditionally it is when the soil reaches a certain temperature. Each area of the country has its own time frame for the application of pre-emergent. For example, the Midwest states are required to put it down in late April to the first week in May.

In central North Carolina this week is a good time to get it out. Pre-emergent is applied for one reason and one reason alone. Pre-emergent is put on lawns to prevent weeds from appearing. If weeds have landed in the soil, pre-emergent kills them before they reach maturity. However, if a yard is left untreated, weeds will not only germinate, they will grow and reseed and take over an entire yard. In a very short period of time, if a yard is not treated with pre-emergent at the right time, you will have a yard filled with unwanted weeds. These weeds will rob the natural grass of nutrients and choke out the blades of grass which provides the beauty to a lawn. I got the pre-emergent out on that Sunday afternoon and applied it to the front yard, the side lot, the front porch section and the back yard. It will not be the last application of pre-emergent but it is a huge step towards the goal of having a strong, beautiful and weedfree lawn.

Every one of us must do the same in our own spiritual lives. We must apply pre-emergent on a regular basis. We must totally cover the front yard of our lives with pre-emergent. We must apply it to the front section of our yard as well. Some would say that the front yard section are those outward actions which everyone sees. Additionally, we must apply it to the side lots of our lives. Many would say that those are the relationships which everyone experiences. Lastly, we must apply pre-emergent to the backyard of our life. These would be the things which no one sees. The backyard is the place where only you see. It is the yard which reveals who you are when no one is looking. It is our inward and most personal parts.

If we are going to prevent weeds from growing into our lives, choking out everything that is good, tainting our landscape with unwanted thorns and thistles, we must apply the pre-emergent before they sprout up. You may be asking what is this pre-emergent that addresses all such areas of my life? What is this pre-emergent which can protect, prevent, and help to insure beauty for all to enjoy? Is this possible? Is there such an application available that can be applied to a person, to a child of God, to a life exposed to weeds which are constantly blowing in the air looking for places to land? The answer to all of these questions is yes. There is an application available. However, it cannot be found at the Home Depot. It is not at Lowes or even at Ace Hardware. This pre-emergent is very close. In fact, for many it may be only a few steps away from you right now. Each day you probably walk past this bag of pre-emergent. It is already poured into the drop-spreader. All what has to be done is for you to apply it onto the spiritual lawn of your life. The pre-emergent which I am referring to is the Word of God. The Word of God, if applied consistently, faithfully and believing in its author, you will throw out a wall of defense against the weeds of life.

So I ask you this day, when was the last time that you seriously put down a layer of pre-emergent onto your life? We need to do it daily. Really, we need to do it moment by moment. We need to do it when any thought with weed potential blows into our life. II Corinthians 10:5 says "We demolish arguments and every pretension that sets itself up against the knowledge of God, and we take captive every thought to make it obedient to Christ." Colossians 3:16 says "Let the Word of Christ dwell in you richly..."

Is the Word dwelling in you richly? Or in another way, is the Word of God being laid across your life thoroughly? If you are applying the spiritual pre-emergent, the Word of God, then you will be preventing lots of weeds or bitter roots from growing. This is our call. This is our place. We are the turf managers of our lives. Let's be faithful in this task each and every day. I will be striving to use my drop spreader every day. I will be praying that you are working your lawn as well. Let's not only prevent some weeds this week, let's do what we need to do in order to grow a beautiful lawn which can serve and testify before a watching and hurting world.

Scripture reading: Hebrews 12:15

Draw near to God and He will draw near to you.

Man's Best Friend

After dinner each evening there is a routine that takes place in our household. I need it to happen and when I take time to do it I cannot wait to do it again. It is a time when I step outside, look up at the stars and hang out with man's best friend. Every evening there is a friend who is the focal point of this routine. Beginning when I walk in the door, this friend of mine has been waiting for an opportunity to be together with me all day long. This friend has been patient through my distractions at work, my hurried lunch routines and my oftentimes disregard when I walk out and return through the front door. This friend of mine is always patient through the greeting of my wife; patient with my catch up time with my son and patient all during dinner. However, when dinner is over, this friend of mine knows that it could be our time. However after dinner, many times there are chores that need to get done. The table has to be cleared, the dishes need to be put away, and the trash must be taken out. Oftentimes several other tasks surface as well. Finally, when all of the priorities of life are accomplished, obligations are taken care of as well as the many things that seem to creep in are performed; I then find time to open the door and spend time with man's best friend.

I have a question for you today. How do you treat mankind's best friend? How do you approach your best friend at the beginning of the day, the middle of the day and the end of the day? What do you do when your very best friend has been waiting for you, calling to you and longing to be with you? Are you like me? Do you make your very best friend the last option of the day? When all of the tasks of life are accomplished, do you then fit Him in? I am not talking about an animal. I am talking about the one who spoke animals, plants, air, water, sun, moon and stars into existence. I am talking about our loving, our all-knowing, our merciful, our most kind, most gracious Heavenly Father. He is the best friend that you and I will ever know. I am talking about the one who created you, the one who designed your face, who sculpted you body and the one who knows you better than you know yourself. I am talking about the one who was in heaven over 2000 years ago. I am speaking of the one who left heaven, was born of a virgin, was sinless, died on a cross and rose on the third day, just for you. I am talking about the most holy, most awesome, and most all powerful God of all creation. He is the one who has been waiting for me each evening. He is the one who has been patiently waiting for me while I do what I selfishly want to do.

Don't do what I all too often do. Don't wait until you step out on the back porch and look to heaven to love and worship your Heavenly Father. He is worthy to be praised from sun up until sun down. He does not only want to be your very best friend, He wants to be the Lord of your life. Your life is like a throne and He wants to be the one who sits on it. He knows what is best for you. Follow Him when you get up in the morning, throughout the day and when you come home in each evening. He is my best friend. He can be your best friend as well. He is man's best friend.

Scripture reading: John 15:15. "I no longer call you servants, because a servant does not know his master's business. Instead, I have called you friends, for everything that I learned from my Father I have made known to you."

Draw near to God and He will draw near to you.

Getting Away

Every year, most every person strives to find some way to get away. Work and obligations oftentimes rise to such a feverish pitch that we just need to go someplace different. These getaways can range from the very simple to the extremely complex. For some, this escape from the pressures of life may be just a stroll downstairs, collapsing in the favorite sofa and mindlessly surf the television. For others, the getaway may be more involved with a car ride across town, an excursion to the mountains, or maybe even a cruise to some far away destination. No matter what the mode of expression, the reasons for the time away seem to always fall into one of the two following categories.

First, we need to find a place where we don't have to think about the stresses, the lists and the deadlines of life. Or, we have an area of our life that has gotten so out of balance that we need to get away to address it. The everyday schedule of life has kept us moving ahead without concern for balance and we just cannot ignore it any longer. For those of us sensing the smothering of life or the scale being tipped completely out of balance, we finally get to a point where we have to do something about it. Usually that involves getting away. Some of us are very fortunate in that time away breaks are already scheduled for us, like Christmas or Summer academic breaks. For others, if it is going to be a part of our life, we need to make it happen ourselves.

Each of our lives as human beings are complex and multi-dimensional. These dimensions basically include the big five. They are the physical, the emotional, the relational or social, the intellectual and the spiritual. Each of these dimensions cries out for attention. If one neglects one of these dimensions, then something usually happens in that person's life. If one of these dimensions is neglected, oftentimes one or more of the other dimensions are affected as well. However, for the one sensitive to these dimensions and their roles in our lives, he or she oftentimes stops, pulls away and addresses the need.

For example, if the physical dimension has been ignored then a decision is needed to address it. If it is not addressed, extra pounds show up, weak bones result, flexibility is reduced and various heart and blood pressure issues surface. If our relational dimension of life is set on the back burner, then the social support system so desperately needed is absent. If the relational dimension of life is neglected, not only does the individual suffer but also those who this person connects with will suffer as well. There are countless examples of relational neglect. Some include the husband neglecting the wife; the dad neglecting the daughter, the son neglecting the grandparents and the sister neglecting the brother. Most of these challenges could be addressed if one would just get away. Getting away is statement that some help is needed. All of life's dimensions are important and necessary. However, there is one dimension which holds both value in this world and the next. Of course, this is the spiritual dimension of life.

The spiritual dimension is the dimension which addresses our relationship with the Lord. Some would interpret the spiritual dimension as the sphere where one finds meaning but I believe it is much more specific than that interpretation. The spiritual dimension of life is your personal relationship with the Lord Jesus. Similar to the physical and relational dimensions previously mentioned, the spiritual dimension can show signs of neglect as well. How can you tell if you have neglected your spiritual dimension or most specifically your walk with the Lord? In the physical dimension, it is much simpler. For one, neglect can be found when you step onto the bathroom scale. In the relational side of life, you can read neglect when your son constantly asking for the car keys with absolutely no interest in you tagging along. But what about the spiritual dimension? How can you tell if you have been ignoring it? What are some signs that inform you that you are in need of a get away?

I believe there are a few key indicators as to whether one is fading in his spiritual walk with the Lord. First of all, there is no desire to talk to the Lord. The person drifting in his walk does not pray to the Lord throughout the day. He feels that he is the captain of his own soul, pulls his own boot straps up and feels no need to call upon the Lord for His will, His insights or His strength. The second sign of a spiritual life in decline has to do with the person's desire to study the Word of God. The Word is never a part of this person's daily reading materials, never is a part of his study priorities and never is a filter through which he interprets the world. It is a book which collects dust and is not important in his life. Third, and more obvious to see than prayer and bible study, is the lack of a desire to be with God's people. The person faltering in his spiritual walk does not make fellowship with his brothers and sisters in Christ a priority. This person rarely attends bible studies, hardly ever goes to church and is really embarrassed when he sees Christians praying, meeting together and talking of the things of God. Lastly, a clear indication that one's spiritual life is in need of repair is the lack of a desire to share it with others. The person falling on the scale of spiritual intimacy with Christ has no desire to tell others of the gospel. He has no burden for those outside of Christ. He has no burden in his heart for those friends, acquaintances and family still trapped in their sins. He is calloused and indifferent to their spiritual need of the Lord.

Someone once said that the Christian life is three steps forward and sometimes two steps back. In other words, when we are moving forward we may fail at times but overall we are still growing in our faith. Our spiritual lives cannot remain flat lined. They are either moving up or they are moving in the other direction. I ask you this day. Which direction are you going? Are you growing in your faith? Are you praying? Are you reading the Word? Are you meeting and enjoying fellowship with other believers? Are you talking of Him to others through your life and words? Of all of the dimensions in life, the most important dimension is our spiritual dimension. The word says "For what does it profit a man to gain the whole world and forfeit his soul."

Please do try to plan a getaway sometime soon where you can reset the balance and get a break from the various stresses of life. However, if at all possible, as you rest those bones and recharge your mental batteries please be intentional in spending time with the Lord. He wants us to get away with Him not just when we request vacation but every day.

Scripture reading: Matthew 6:5-6

Draw near to God and He will draw near to you.

Roots Run Deep

I just finished working two solid days in the yard. I spent all day Saturday and a several hours in the afternoon on Sunday doing some necessary yard work. I mowed the front and the back, used the weed eater on the side of the house against the flower beds and broke out the blower moving some leftover leaves from the fall. After all of that, I transported several loads of limbs and rotten blocks of wood down to the road for the coming roadside pickup. Even though these yard work tasks may seem mundane and arduous to you, it was pure joy to me. Nevertheless, even though I really do enjoy most everything having to do with yardwork, there was one task that I did not look forward to doing. Because it is every growing and everpresent, I can never fully call it a day until I work on this area at least a little. Some of you may be guessing what chore that I am speaking of. Some of you may have some experience with yard work and know of the chore that is forever lurking just off the mowed surfaces of the yard. Yes, this last chore was the green leaved nemesis is always there no matter how hard you try to beat it back.

Of course I am speaking of the kudzu weed. This time of year, kudzu has to be addressed for if one waits too long into the summer it may be too late. This past Saturday and Sunday, I went after my yard's stand of kudzu. If I did not do it then I definitely will not want do it in mid-July with temperatures possibly reaching 95 degrees with 90% humidity. Saturday and Sunday seemed appropriate to take it on. It was cool and windy. The soil was wet and soft and it was time. It was time to put my back into something that needed to be taken care of. I did not clear all of it but I made a dent in a battle which only time will tell as to who the victor shall be.

Kudzu is a weed that covers non-mowed areas in the south like a western wildfire. Here are some interesting facts about this weed which has been climbing, sprawling and infesting much of my backyard for years now. According to Kudzuworld.com, Kudzu (Pueraria lobata) was brought to the United States in 1876 for a Japanese Exposition in Philadelphia, and it basically "escaped." In Japan it generally grows like a normal plant, however the American South is a perfect climate for it. Introducing Kudzu was like introducing a match to gasoline, and the results can now be easily seen. The Japanese love it, but it grows at a normal pace in Japan. In the American South, it's a predator.

- It grows more than 7 feet (more than 2 meters) a week. Almost nothing can stop it.
- It takes 10 to 15 years to control a Kudzu patch – even with chemicals. Effective herbicides are napalm and agent orange but they often destroy the soil. Of 12 known soil friendly herbicides, 10 have no effect, and 2 make it grow better.
- Its covers more than 2.8 million square km of the American South. Patches often are 6+ miles long.
- It's even been called "The vegetable form of cancer."

So how do you get rid of it? If chemicals hardly phase it, what can be done? Since I do not want to kill the soil with chemicals and cannot afford to do that method anyway, there is only one thing that can be done to take care of kudzu. I have to get the shovel out, do some loosing up and stretching, and get to work. Yes, you guessed it. I have to dig to the root. I have to dig as far down as I can and get every last portion of the root. If I do not get it all, it will be back and attack my yard with the same intensity as it had before. So Saturday and Sunday I dug and dug trying desperately to get to the very bottom of the root to as many plants as I could. I knew that success would only happen when I reached the bottom of the root and scraped out every portion of the kudzu.

I could not cut the leaves or even the stem just below the surface. I had to dig deep and make sure that the full root was gone. If I did not get it, it might take a while but slowly and surely it would make its way back to the surface. It would then begin its leather like creeping vines and expand its blanketing coverage making its presence known in my yard once again. I went to work on this final chore on those two weekend days. I was exhausted but hopeful that I got to the root of many kudzu plants.

In similar fashion, our Lord wants us to find the root of something in our lives. Our all-knowing, all powerful and all loving Heavenly Father wants us to find the root of something else which can spread out of control in our lives. We cannot get at it with chemicals. We cannot dig to it with shovels. Hard work and sweat on the brow would never pull it totally out. What is this invasive object and how then can we get rid of it?

The book of Hebrews in the New Testament talks of this root which has to be laid aside. "Therefore we also, since we are surrounded by so great a cloud of witnesses, let us lay aside every weight, and the sin which so easily ensnares us, and let us run with endurance the race that is set before us." Heb. 12:1, 2. The Lord wants us to get rid of the sin which so easily ensnares us.

Until we go home to be with the Lord, we will have sinful desires to deal with. Ephesians 4 speaks more on this but calls it the old man. "But you have not so learned Christ, if indeed you have heard Him and have been taught by Him, as the truth is in Jesus: that you put off, concerning your former conduct, the old man which grows corrupt according to deceitful lusts, and be renewed in the spirit of your mind, and that you put on the new man which was created according to God, in true righteousness and holiness."

So here we have it, the Lord not only wants us to dig out the kudzu but He wants us to plant something back in its place, the new man. So, what is this new man and how do we get it? How do we lay aside sin which entangles and put off this sinful nature? We do it by putting on Christ. Putting on Christ is putting your faith and trust in the Lord Jesus Christ to be your savior and your Lord. II Corinthians 5:17 tells us what will be the result if we do this. We will not only be pulling out a bad root, the old man, He will make us a new creation. "Therefore, if anyone is in Christ, he is a new creation, old things have passed away; behold, all things have become new."

If you have decided to follow Jesus, not only will the root of sin be out of the yard, you will have a new heart. Ezekiel 36:26 says "I will give you a new heart and put a new spirit within you; I will take your heart of stone out of your flesh and give you a heart of flesh." Will we still sin? Yes. Will we still make bad choices? Yes. However, the difference then will be that God is in us. Instead of a root growing wild, out of control, covering every aspect of our life, the Lord Jesus will be in your life and doing a work. The root of sin will be gone.

Upon receiving Christ, our job will be to feed the new spiritual plant within us. We are to water the spiritual fruit tree in our life. This is done by ingesting the pure Word of God. If we do this, we will bear the fruit of love, joy, peace, patience, kindness and self control. It is a whole new ball game when Jesus becomes a part of your life. He is the farmer who did the digging. We are now the servant who can decide which plants get attention, the old sin nature or the new man.

There is only one cure for the root of sin in our lives and His name is Jesus. Look around. Spiritual kudzu, called sin is ruling and taking over many lives. It is a covering which is so smothering that many cannot truly see life as it is supposed to be seen. You do have the answer. Pray for them. Love on them. Be their friend. And then maybe someday if the time is right and they are ready to hear, tell them about the only one who can give a life which is full and meaningful. Tell them about a life which is heaven bound and not enslaved to the root of sin.

Scripture reading: Romans 11:16

Draw near to God and He will draw near to you.

Audit Joy

Many years ago, I had breakfast with the current Head Coach of the Detroit Lions. Two years earlier he was with the Baltimore Ravens as their offensive coordinator. He made all of the play calls for the quarterback of the Ravens who went on to win the Super Bowl and game MVP. Jim Caldwell is his name. Our memorable talk occurred at the IHOP which used to be right next to the Wake Forest University campus. We talked of many things that morning. One thing that we talked about was his team's profanity box that he set up. I listened to how he had his players and coaches pay money into the profanity box if they spoke profanity on the field of play. He said that the fines were not that much for the players but it was pretty sizeable for the coaches, which was understandable. However, for himself, if he were ever to speak a word of profanity in or around the field of play, his fine was much greater. He told me that his fine was $1,000 for voicing one word of profanity. As far as I know, Jim Caldwell never paid into the box. He was confident in who he was as a man, a Christian man. He made a rule and made his penalty many times greater than all of the others. He was the leader. He set the example and if he were ever to break it, it would cost him the most. Jim Caldwell is a man of integrity. His confidence came from his life as a Christian. I have never forgotten that breakfast.

Besides the story of the profanity box, Mr. Caldwell shared many other things that morning that have stuck with me. Of his many encouraging words, he said one thing that stood out above the rest. He told me a phrase that I have thought about many times since our breakfast that morning. This phrase came to my mind a few days back. It came to my mind as I greeted by our university's auditor of operations. Jim Caldwell told me something that rang in my ears as I smiled and shook our auditor's hand. Jim Caldwell told me this. He said, "Max, an honest man never minds being checked."

At 1:30pm on the day in question, a sharped dressed man in a suit and tie came into my office. He sat down, pulled out a large folder and thumbed through the stack until he came to my name and my department on it. He handed me a copy, took a deep breath and began his audit. For the next hour I sat before this gentleman and answered every question that he asked of me. I showed him documents, procedural forms and shared operational protocol on the topics in which he was keenly interested. At the end of the time, he stood up, thanked me for my time, shook my hand and left. At 2:32, I returned to my desk, sat back in my chair and recalled the words of a friend from years past. "Max, an honest man never minds being checked."

So after another week has been crammed with work, a month full of numerous decisions and a year of mileage on your life tires, do you mind being checked? How have you done? Like Mr. Caldwell's profanity box, has the box which you have set up for others been backed up by your own words, your own thoughts and your own actions? If a 'relationship with the Lord' auditor were to show up at your door, what would he find in the records concerning your walk with Christ? Would the greeting be filled with shock, shame and fear? Or would it be audit joy?

As we know, the Lord is there when no one is looking. The Lord knows our every thought. The Lord knows when we have cut a corner, stretched the truth or told a flat out lie. He knows when we have been dishonest, unethical, underhanded, mean, revengeful, lazy or gluttonous. He knows if we have stolen time, stolen an object, or stolen from a person's dignity. However, He

163

also knows when we have loved, when we have given of ourselves and when we have been kind, tenderhearted and fair. He knows when we have put others ahead of ourselves, when we have spoken words of encouragement and when we have worked hard, as hard as we possibly could work. The Lord asks us to audit ourselves. In I Corinthians 11: 28 the Lord says "A man ought to examine himself." And in Lamentations 3:40 "Let us examine our ways and test them."

As you continue this week, I challenge you to remember the words of Mr. Caldwell. "An honest man never minds being checked." If we have been honest with ourselves, honest with others and honest with the Lord God Almighty, we will have true joy in living. We will have audit joy.

Finish strong and remember this one thing. If the box is full of intentional rebellion or you have not been honest, I John 1:9 is there for you. It is there for me. It says " If we confess our sins, He is faithful and just to forgive us our sins and cleanse us from all unrighteousness." Jesus paid it all. All to Him I owe. Sin had left a crimson stain. He washed it white as snow.

Scripture reading: Proverbs 16:11

Draw near to God and He will draw near to you.

Awake at the Wheel

Looking through the rear view mirror on a long car ride home the other day, I saw a wonderful site. I saw my oldest son, youngest son and youngest daughter with their eyes closed. They were fast asleep. Gazing to my right I looked over into the passenger seat and I viewed my beautiful wife of 25 years asleep as well. The car was quiet, the road was smooth and there I was behind the wheel with my wife and children fast asleep. I was at the wheel and for a moment thought about who I was carrying down the road towards our destination. In my care was precious and priceless cargo. I was tired from the day's adventures but the weariness did not punch through my gaze which was fixed on the road.

I too was up until 1am watching a movie. I too was up early doing ride after ride, climbing multiple flights of stairs at an indoor waterpark. I too walked around an outlet mall for nearly four hours watching and giving nods of approval for the needed acquisitions. I was tired but something much greater than my physical state helped me to stay awake at the wheel. You see, I love my family beyond words. I know how blessed I am to have such a privilege and responsibility of having them in my care. I had to be alert. I had to me watchful. I could not for one moment lose my focus on the road. Not for one moment could I let my physical tiredness, my mental focus and my total commitment drift. For the entire drive home, I had to be awake at the wheel. Their very lives and their future were in my hands at that moment. It was up to me not to fall asleep. I was tired but a greater strength supported me. I had a strength that was rooted in a desire to care for them beyond my personal desires for rest.

I wanted to be there for them. I had to be there. Others, many others were depending on me as well to be awake at the wheel.

I need to ask you something this day. I need to ask you about something that you too have been asked to carry. I need to ask you whether you have been awake at the wheel while carrying such precious cargo. You see, the Lord God almighty has entrusted you with something which is more valuable than all the gold in the Yukon Territory. The Lord has entrusted you with something that is more lucrative than all of the oil in the oil fields of the Persian Gulf. The Lord has given you something to carry which is worth more than all of the real estate, all of the stock portfolios, and all of the material possessions mankind has ever possessed. You see, the Lord has entrusted you with something that is priceless. It is beyond calculation. It is immeasurable. What is this which is so worthy of our focus, so worthy of our continual concentration, so worthy for us to deny ourselves even of rest? What is this thing which every distraction must be set aside for, every motive must be filtered through and every action must be weighed against? What can be so valuable, so important, that our very life must be put on the line to defend and to guard it?

This thing which God has given us which I believe we must carry and protect with all that we have is this: A personal relationship with Jesus Christ. Having and keeping a close personal relationship with the Lord Jesus Christ is the most valuable thing that we will ever possess. I encourage you to do everything that is necessary to protect your walk with Jesus. Stay alert. Stay focused. Don't get distracted. Don't run off the road and down the wrong path. Definitely don't cross the center line. Stay awake at the wheel. Look around constantly. Be circumspect. Remember, our fleshly temptations, the enticements of the world and even Satan himself wants us to forget about this cargo. And even though it is sad to say, many among us are doing this very thing. They are forgetting what they are carrying in the car. Be strong. Don't let it happen to you. Don't let a story be told that you fell asleep at the wheel and hurt this priceless possession which we are privileged to enjoy. Remember, " For God so loved the world that He gave His only begotten Son, that whoever believes in Him should not perish but have everlasting life."

We can only do this with the Lord's help. Therefore, do not put out the Spirits fire. Do not quench the Spirit. Do not grieve the Spirit. Instead, be filled with the Spirit. Instead, keep in step with the Spirit. As you may or may not know, the Spirit (the Holy Spirit/God Himself) does His work in our lives by the confession of our own selfish control, rebellion and sin and by the constant ingestion of His Holy Word.

We have the privilege of walking in newness of life. We have the honor of having a personal relationship with Jesus. As Ephesians 4:1 says "As a prisoner for the Lord, then, I urge you to live a life worthy of the calling you have received." Let's walk worthy.

Let's be Awake at the Wheel of the relationship which is more valuable than anything we will ever know or possess. Let's strive to treat it as such.

Scripture reading: I Peter 5:8

Draw near to God and He will draw near to you.

One Shining Life

For the past 24 years, every March my wife and I look forward to the end of the NCAA Men's Division I national championship basketball game. Every year after the final horn sounds, after the interviews are done and after the nets are cut down and the trophies handed out, CBS puts together something which we thoroughly enjoy watching. It is called "One Shining Moment." It is a video montage of the tournament coupled with a song from Luther Vandross. It shows scenes from the start of the tournament to the end of the tournament. It will show short video clips ranging from coaches' intense expressions to players exuberant displays of joy on down to despondent sighs of disappointment, disbelief and game ending sadness. We have watched this "One shining moment" when Duke won back to back national championships, when Florida repeated and won back to back to last year when Louisville won its third overall in the history of the school. Regardless of how competitive the game is or whether we have a favorite in the game, we always watch the game to get to the end so we can enjoy the 'One Shining Moment.'

When very fortunate outstanding players get to play in any championship game, they get one shining moment. It is only for a moment and then it is gone. They get to shine on a major stage and then it is over. It's a moment that they will never forget and for most will never have a chance to see again. It will be 'One Shining Moment'.

Like these elite athletes who received one shining moment on a basketball court in a huge dome in the NCAA basketball national championship game, we too will receive something that is bright

168

and shining. However, we will receive it but it will not be for a moment.

The holy bible reveals to us that if we have trusted in the Lord Jesus Christ as our Lord and Savior, we have received a light that never goes out. In Psalms 27:1 the psalmist writes "The Lord is my light and salvation; whom shall I fear?" Other scriptures tell that we continually possess this light as we go about our day to day lives. Isaiah 2:5 says "...come and let us walk in the light of the Lord." And then in other places of scripture the Lord challenges us to not only possess this light and walk around with it, He urges us to let it out for others to see. Matthew 5:16 says "Let your light so shine before men that they may see your good works and glorify your Father in heaven." When we let this light shine, scripture says that we will illuminate the world. Ephesians says "you are light in the Lord. Walk as children of the light."

Brothers/sisters, we are to shine as lights in a world desperately looking for answers. We are not to be like a 3 hour basketball game with "One Shining Moment." We are to be an example of a new creation, walking in trust and obedience to a loving Lord, one shining moment after another, day by day, week by week, month by month, year by year. Philippians gives us this charge and the importance of being "One Shining Life." Philippians 2:15,16a says " ...that you may become blameless and harmless, children of God without fault in the midst of a crooked and perverse generation, among whom you shine as lights in the world, holding fast the word of life,..."

So this very day as you put your hands to the many things in front of you, may it not be just a moment of time and shining for only for a second. May all of our lives be a continuous reflection of the light which has been indwelt in our hearts for a needy world to see. Run the race. Fight the good fight. Keep the faith.

And most of all, glorify our Lord Jesus Christ in everything that we say, feel, think and do. For in so doing, we will be "One Shining Life" which will make a difference in the circle of influence the Lord has given us.

Scripture reading: Hebrews 12:1

Draw near to God and He will draw near to you.

Render Unto Caesar

Eventually, whether you are ready or not, whether you want to or not, a certain day of the year will eventually loom large for you every spring. This day has to be kept in mind from January 1st until December 31st. It is a day that you will need to plan for, budget for, create files for and mentally prepare for every April. This day is always in the middle of national political debates, continually discussed when pay stubs are issued and always dreaded when the day finally arrives. This day if ignored can possibly embarrass a family, it can financially penalize if put off and if blatant enough, ignoring this day could send an individual to prison. The day that I am talking about is April 15, the day that we as citizens of the United States of America pay our taxes to the Internal Revenue Service. A few don't mind this day but the vast majority cannot wait until the day has clicked to April 16. I am one of the latter.

Paying taxes is a fact of life. We enjoy certain services from our city, state and federal government so it is only fair that we pay our fair share to support those services. Such services include: the local police, the fire department, trash collection and disposal, street cleaning and clearing in cases of inclement weather, parks and recreation, various social services, the public libraries, the public schools, the public fairgrounds, sanitation and sewer, water supply and of course our public servants like the city council, mayor, city manager, legislatures, armed forces, national guard etc. As you can see, our tax dollars are asked to do a lot and we should expect that our monies are spent wisely and for the public good. Because of these needed services, there is a portion of my check each month and another portion of my checkbook each April which belongs to the city, state and federal government.

Our tax dollars must be paid or rendered to those in governmental leadership. In many ways the monies paid to them belong to them. When we render to these governmental agencies, we are pay them back, implying a debt that we truly owe. We are obligated to pay these taxes. It is our ethical and moral responsibility no matter which party is sitting in power.

There is another rendering that is very similar to the rendering that every US citizen must acknowledge each April 15. However this rendering does not take place on one day during the year. This rendering takes place every day of the year, every 365 of them. This rendering was discussed many years ago during a conversation between the Pharisees and Jesus. It is found in the gospel of Matthew Chapter 22:15-21.

"Then the Pharisees (religious rulers of the day) went and plotted how they might entangle Him(Jesus) in His talk. Tell us, therefore, what do You think? Is it lawful to pay taxes to Caesar or not?" But Jesus perceived their wickedness, and said, "Why do you test Me, you hypocrites? Show Me the tax money." So they brought Him a denarius. And He said to them, "Whose image and inscription is this?" They said to Him, "Caesar's." And He said to them, "Render therefore to Caesar the things that are Caesar's, and to God the things that are God's."

Rendering unto Caesar (in our day the government), what is owed is necessary and right. Paul wrote in Romans this very thing. "Let every person be in subjection to the governing authorities. For there is no authority except from God, and those which exist are established by God....Render to all what is due them; tax to whom tax is due; custom to whom custom; fear to whom fear; honor to whom honor." And Peter addressed it as well saying in I Peter 2:13-15. "Submit yourselves for the Lord's sake to every human institution, whether to a king as one in authority, or to governors as sent by him for the punishment of evildoers and the praise of those who do right. For such is the will of God that by doing right you may silence the ignorance of foolish men."

We are to render to the government what is the governments' and we are to render to God what is God's. The question is this: What is God's? If we are obligated to give to the local government what is theirs, what are we obligated to give to God? What is His? What is God's? What does He own? What is He in charge of? What belongs to Him? The answer is obvious. Everything is His. He owns everything. He is in charge of everything. Everything belongs to Him. What do I mean here? Well, He created the earth; therefore all that is in the earth belongs to Him. He created you therefore you belong to Him. Earth, moon, sun, stars, plants, animals, mountains, seas, plains, He owns it all. We are only stewards put in charge of His creation to manage it.

There are figurative and literal thrones built all around the world. The Lord Jesus is to sit as Lord on all of them. He is the Lord God Almighty, king of all creation. He is to sit on every throne. However there is one throne where someone else starts out in life sitting on it. This throne belongs to God but someone else is on it. It is the throne of an individual's life.

Many a men and women since birth and by deliberate rebellion have put themselves on this throne. This throne belongs to the Lord. He is looking for men and women everywhere, in every land, of every race, to get off this throne and give it back to the only One who is supposed to be sitting on it. The Lord Jesus is calling mankind to give Him His throne back. Will you give it back to Him? Have you given it back to Him? If you have then you have rendered to God what is God's. All things and every area of life belong to God. Will you give it to Him?

If you have never have given your life to Jesus and feel that you are still sitting on the throne of your life, then I would like to encourage you to give the throne back to Jesus, even this very day. Render unto Caesar what is Caesar's but much more importantly render unto to God what is God's. An old hymn speaks of a person who decided to render unto God what is God's:

All to Jesus I surrender
All to Him I freely give
I will ever love and trust Him
In His presence daily live
I surrender all, I surrender all

All to Thee my blessed Savior
I surrender all

Let's render unto God what is God's.

Draw near to God and He will draw near to you.

90 Mile Per Hour Arm

When I was in college, I used to play left field on the varsity baseball team. During infield I would never skip the ball to 2nd base or to 3rd base. I would fire it all the way to the base on a line and in the air. When throwing to home, I could throw in the air but would lower my sites slightly so the 3rd baseman could cut it off if needed. My throw would consistently be a one hop shot from left field. I had what some would say was a powerful arm from left field. When finally clocked I discovered that I had a 90 mile per hour arm. God was the source of this gift and I am thankful for the opportunities I enjoyed because of it.

These days, my arm is much different. Instead of throwing bullets across a field on a line or firing strikes passed hitters from the mound, my arm and capacities are much different. At this very point, I cannot raise my arm in a complete circle, pain is in my shoulder when I move it in certain directions and I cannot throw a ball 30 feet let alone even 60 feet back to a pitcher's mound. What happened? Why is playing catch and throwing it back to my son or daughter a nearly impossible task? Why is it a very real possibility that I may never be able to throw again with the velocity that I had just a year ago? Though age does have something to do with it, the bulk of my arm's demise started with some advice I received in a fitness discussion about a year ago.

Fitness is a craze in not only this country but around the world. The benefits of exercise are well documented and all of us should be participating in regular exercise. However, before we undertake such activity, we need to make sure that the instructions communicated are solid and that our work-out routine will support our fitness goals. As in my case, neither was done. I performed activities with my shoulders on a regular basis which was tearing down my arm and its capacity to throw. The routines that I chose, actually worked against my desire to continue throwing. Therefore, when I was asked to play catch, my arm gave out resulting in the state that I am currently in. I am optimistic however. I do hope that I will be able to get movement back. But it is a very good possibility that I will not be able to ever throw like I did before taking the advice that I listened to a year ago.

Why do I mention this on this glorious day that the Lord has given? Why do I bring up such a story of struggle and disappointment? Why do I share what once was and which now is not possible? I share this because this all could have been avoided. Though I never will be back at the 90 mph clip that I was able to perform years ago, I still could have been firing darts to my children on the ball field or in the batting cage. My throwing career did not have to result in catching the ball, flipping it to another who then throws it back for me. This was all very preventable. The life I am now experiencing could have been different. My arm strength could still be intact if I just would not have listened to the opinions of non-qualified instructors. My capability to someday pitch to my grandchildren (Lord willing) could still have been there. Nevertheless, I will go through the therapy and will hope for the best. However, I do wonder if I just would have listened and stayed with the old ways; if I just would have stayed with the fitness teaching which I was raised with. I wonder if only I would have relied on the baseball teaching that I used when I used to whip the ball all around a baseball diamond. If only I would have stayed with what I had known and never left.

Our walks with the Lord are very similar to my shoulder. The Old Book, the Bible, has given us instruction on how to live this life. God's Word has revealed to us ways to approach the various issues which will confront us in life. The Holy Scriptures have had a long standing spiritual exercise plan that will not only maintain those gifts that we were born with, but it will actually enhance and grow the spiritual gifts which we have received from on-high.

So, when the latest fashion, the latest technique, the latest life routine or philosophy comes along promising success, be careful. Be careful not to do like I did with my arm a year ago. Be careful not to take the teaching hook, line and sinker. If you do, you may find yourself being less than your full potential, less than your very best, all the while staring at a future which is not all what it can be. Filter the counsel that you receive from culture, from teachers, and from friends. Check them against the old ways handed down to us from the Lord God Almighty. Check all of these new life training, life preparing techniques against the words given to us many years ago. If you do, you will be in a better position to make decisions and live a life on a scale which our loving Lord desires of you/of me.

I listened to bad counsel and am now paying the price physically. With the spiritual dimension, which is so the more important, may we all check it against the pure, steadfast, immoveable, rock of the Word of God. If we do, then our spiritual arms will stay strong, our spiritual futures will remain hopeful and our life possibilities will continue to be all which they should be.

Scripture reading: I Peter 2:2

Draw near to God and He will draw near to you.

The Mirror

This morning I woke up, stumbled to the bathroom, turned on the light and gazed into the mirror. I was a frightening sight this morning. My hair was in a huge mess, I needed to shave and my eyes had some severe bags underneath them. I would have been fine if I had skipped the glance but I just had to look into the mirror. I probably would have gone about my morning much happier and much more confident in my appearance but I decided to look into the mirror. You see the mirror shows you as you really look. It doesn't dress things up at all. It basically tells it like it is.

I don't particularly like mirrors but I know that I need them. I would feel better about myself not knowing my appearance but mirrors make me better. Because of a mirror in our bathroom, I am able to make adjustments. I am able to comb my hair, shave my face, wipe the sleep out of my eyes, splash some water on my face, take a shower and face the day. The mirror gave me the opportunity this morning to make a change. It gave me an opportunity to see myself as I really am and make an adjustment. I can look into the mirror and forget what I look like or I can gaze into it, see myself as I really am and do things differently.

People can be like mirrors as well. I found that out the other day. A few days back I had lunch with a young man who was a mirror. Through his words and descriptions he told me how I really was. He told me how I looked before others. He told me how I sounded. He told me where I was wrong, where I was weak. He told me when I appeared judgmental. He told me when I made myself look unreal. He told me when I appeared less than I could be. Though he never held up a 6 foot tall by 3 foot wide mirror, he was the mirror. He explained and showed me how I looked in the morning, how I looked during the day, how I looked in public, how I looked in small groups. It was not a very pleasant experience.

Part of me wanted to make an excuse for every behavioral hair that was out of place. Part of me wanted to find a reason for the insensitivity and judgment that I cast upon individuals but I could not. I listened and observed from this human mirror a sight that I needed to see. Did I want to hear about my misspoken words? Did I want to hear about a lack of connection with those whom I often speak? Did I want to see myself making judgments that only God should be making? No, I did not. However, it was good for me to see it in this mirror. It was good for me to hear it. Now, after gazing into this mirror, hopefully I will be a better husband, a better dad, a better friend, a better teacher, a better person and a better believer.

As you probably know by now, I see much of life through the lenses of God's words to us. Though I do believe I have a pretty sharp mind, I really do not have it all figured out. On my own I don't know where I came from. On my own I don't know where this life of mine will end up. On my own I don't know why I am here and what will truly make me be a joyful and fulfilled individual. I have read lots of books in my life. I have read many of the classics. I have read biographies. I have read business theory books. I have read generational theory works. Many of them have great insights and oftentimes I take notes from them. However, I am still biased in a certain direction. Though many in this world don't agree with me; though many feel that it was just ordinary men writing stories; though many feel that they are just words; I find that what I draw upon for strength and insight is not just any book. As you probably know I am talking of the bible.

To me the bible is not a book of lists. To me it is not a book of laws and 'thou shalt nots.' To me it is not a bunch of stories with supposed contradictory statements. To me the bible is a love story. To me the bible is a story of how God created us in His image, how He created this world for us, how He wants a relationship with us, how He truly loves us. To me the bible is real, true words of life that can give us hope for our broken and hurting world. To me the bible is God's personal, intimate, comforting, encouraging, and challenging word to guys like me, a stubborn, judgmental, and many times unreal person. To me the bible is different than all other writings of man. Why? Because it isn't just a writing of man, it is God breathed. To me the bible gives me words from my creator who knows and loves me best in spite of my many faults and failures. I don't know why He loves me so, He just does. How do I know this? How do I know He loves me? I learned it a long time ago. I learned it and taught it to all four of my most cherished possessions in all of the world. I learned its truth which was put to a song many years ago. This song was one of the very first songs that I taught my four children. We would sing it many times before we would say our prayers at night. How do I know that he loves me?

"Jesus loves me this I know for the bible tells me so. Little ones to Him belong. They are weak but He is strong. Yes, Jesus loves me. Yes, Jesus loves me. Yes, Jesus loves me. The bible tells me so."

I do apologize if I have ever come across as judgmental, insensitive and unbending. I am an imperfect man and I know that I am imperfect in many things that I say. However, I do care for you all and believe with all my heart that God loves you too. He loves you and really does want you to love Him back.

Nevertheless, He is a gentleman and will not force Himself upon anyone. Love is love when it is chosen and not coerced.

To that young man out there who had lunch with me today I want to say thank you. Thank you for being a mirror and for reminding me of another mirror that I need to gaze into much more often and honestly.

Scripture reading: James 1:23-25 says "Anyone who listens to the word but does not do what it says is like someone who looks at his face in a mirror and, after looking at himself, goes away and immediately forgets what he looks like. But whoever looks intently into the perfect law that gives freedom, and continues in it—not forgetting what they have heard, but doing it—they will be blessed in what they do."

Draw near to God and He will draw near to you.

He's my Friend

I invited a wonderful guy named Jeff along with his wife and family to a church service the week before Easter. It was a musical entitled 'Resurrection Celebration.' Sitting next to my friend, that evening I leaned over and started showing Jeff all of the people who I knew in the production. I pointed up to the stage stating that I knew one of the disciples. I knew Mary in the production. I knew a young man named Joseph as well. After going through most of the names, I went back to the top of the list and I said something which made Jeff and I smile. I told him this: "And David Moore is in the musical as well. David is the owner of the Chick-filet at the intersection of Peacehaven and Robinhood. David Moore is playing Jesus tonight; he is a friend of mine." Right after I said it, Jeff looked at me and gave me a big smile. You see what I said could have been taken in one of two ways. The phrase could have been meant that David Moore is a the friend of mine. It also could have meant that Jesus, who David Moore was playing, is a friend of mine. Repeating it again I said "David Moore is playing Jesus tonight, He is a friend of mine." My intentions were to say that I knew David and that he was a friend. But for that one moment I did realize another thing, Jesus is my friend as well.

In our oftentimes strict viewpoint of our faith, many of us lean heavily on the truth that Jesus is our Savior, which He is. We also believe fully in the truth that He should be the Lord of our lives as well, which He should be. However, there is another truth that we must not ever forget as well. Jesus is our friend. He is closer than a brother. He is a true friend. In John 15:15 Jesus reaffirms this when He states "I no longer call you servants, because a servant does not know his master's business. Instead, I have called you <u>friends,</u> for everything that I learned from my Father I have made known to you." Jesus calls us friends.

How do you look at your faith? Is it a bunch of do's and don'ts? Is it a long list of things to avoid and things to perform? Is it a set of rules, possibly made up by you or others? Or, is it possible that your faith not only acknowledges Jesus as Savior and Lord but also as a friend. Remember, Christianity is not about religion. Christianity is about a relationship with a person. Christianity is a person and His name is Jesus. Just like we know Abraham Lincoln lived, we know Jesus Christ lived. Just like we know all about the talks that Abraham Lincoln gave, so we know all about the words that Jesus spoke. How do you treat Jesus? Do you practice His presence? For example, do you allow Him to be with you while at the dinner table? Is He with you on your nights out? Do you allow Him to be with you in the classroom? How about when watching television when no one else is with you, is He there too? You see Jesus wants to be in every room in our life. He is the friend that is closer than a brother.

Don't let your faith be reduced to a bunch of have to's or do's and don'ts. Don't let your faith be a list of obligations. Let your faith be what it was supposed to be from the very beginning. Our faith is for us to enjoy God and His presence forever. Our faith is to walk with Him, talk with Him and commune with Him in totally transparent friendship moment by moment and day by day. When we pray, it should never be stiff, cold and formal. When we pray, our prayers ought to be real, transparent and honest. He knows our hearts. Why not be open with Him like you would with your best friend? When your faith is a task, then it becomes a burden and you will eventually tire, burnout and run. However, if your faith is an anticipated and enjoyed open relationship with our accepting and loving God, then true life will be lived. When you are afraid, tell Him. When you are tempted, tell Him. When you are angry, tell Him. He will be there for you if only you will let Him.

Scripture reading: John 15:13 says "Greater love has no one than this, that he lay down his life for his friends." Isn't it great that we were the friends He was thinking about?

Draw near to God and He will draw near to you.

The Walking Dead

I cannot believe it. I joined my youngest son and watched two episodes of The Walking Dead the other night. For those who do not know about the show, it is a TV series about some guys and gals trying to get away from walking dead people. If you get bit by one of these walking dead, the disease will eventually kill you and you turn into a zombie looking for others to consume as well. What I did not know before I sat down comfortably in our downstairs sectional couch, was how normal alive people got rid of these zombies. I was not informed that the only way to do away with the walking dead was to kill these creatures. Therefore within minutes of the episode's beginning, I was brought face to face with multiple zombie attacks with many of them finding their end. In a fairly graphic fashion, definitely not appropriate for the young, the main actors in the show defended themselves and killed the walking dead who were after them time and time again.

As you can imagine, this is not a show for the weak in stomach or for young people. Though the storyline was interesting (and I have yet to watch a show since) it was still hard for me to imagine dead people walking around in everyday life. It was difficult for me to picture dead people walking in hospitals, on streets, in office buildings, in parks and in schools. It was hard for me to picture dead people walking.

However, as I watched the show, I realized something that I had not thought of before. I realized something which I had read about before but I had never seen until the other night. I realized that much like the show, there are dead people walking around me each day. Like the show, I realized that there are dead people in the stores with me, on the streets with me and on walking paths with me. Mixed in the dead are alive people in those same locations as well.

Obviously, I am not talking about people with blood stained decaying bodies with outstretched arms making weird sounds and looking for people to consume. I am talking about something else, something much different, and something on the spiritual dimension. I am talking about the spiritual state of many people. Scripture talks of mankind's spiritual state as being either being dead or being alive. Though I never used to feel dead before, I now know that at one time that I was dead, spiritually dead. Only the Lord knows who are alive spiritually and who are currently dead. However, scripture does talk about a transition out of this death, this walking death, and it involves faith in Jesus Christ.

Ephesians 2: 1-5 explains it more clearly. "And you He made alive, who were dead in trespasses and sins, in which you once walked according to the course of this world, according to the prince of the power of the air, the spirit who now works in the sons of disobedience, among whom also we all once conducted ourselves... vs 4. But God, who is rich in mercy, because of His great love with which He loved us, even when we were dead in trespasses, made us alive together with Christ."

You see, in Christ, faith in Christ, we are made spiritually alive. However, if one is still outside of Christ, scripture says that he or she is at the moment dead spiritually. He or she is The Walking Dead. How do we know this? What other scripture speaks of this life and death? I John 5:12, says "He who has the Son (Jesus) has life, he who does not have the Son of God does not have life." and Colossians 2:13 says "And you, being dead in your trespasses and the uncircumcision of your flesh, He (Jesus) has made alive together with Him, having forgiven you all trespasses."

Our place is not to determine who is spiritually dead or who is not. Our job is to let our light shine before others so that they may see our works and give God the glory. We are called to always be ready to give the reason for our hope. May we be thankful this day that the Lord Jesus has made us spiritually alive. As we enter the week set before us, may we all remember the spiritual blessing that we have and to pray for those who are still looking for life. Because He lives, I am alive. I am no longer one of The Walking Dead. May we be the vessels to help others to become alive as well.

Scripture reading: I John 5:12

Draw near to God and He will draw near to you.

Run and Not Be Weary

I don't know if you have ever had one of those days but I did just the other day. I felt tired all day long. I was able to get a lot of work done but I felt like I was pulling a 200 pound sack of sand behind me the entire day. I worked in my office, surveyed activity spaces, ran errands across campus and even visited an event supply store. I was able to chip away at the to-do list for the day but I felt tired the entire time. This is usually not my calling card but that day it was. Whether it was that I was operating on only a few hours sleep, not having a good solid breakfast or not getting in a workout, I don't know. Nevertheless, I was tired and weary. I felt weak and heavy laden. I felt faint. It was not right. We are not meant to feel this way but I did. Maybe you have had one of those days. Maybe you have felt the same way. That was my story just the other day.

On that day I am talking about my physical state of affairs. Mentally I felt sharp. Socially I felt like I was engaged, encouraging and helpful. Intellectually and professionally, I tackled the things that needed tackling. However, I was still physically tired. I was physically less than I could have been. If I were asked to run a half marathon, a 5K or maybe just one mile, I do believe that I would have struggled that day. I was tired, weak, heavy laden and slightly faint. I am hopeful that days like that will be rare. In the future, I will make it a point to get a full night's sleep, drink a tall glass of orange juice, go for a run, take my full dose of vitamins and minerals, and have a hearty bowl of oatmeal. If I do these things I am confident that I will get back on track.

However, in thinking about that rough day, I do wonder about the spiritual part of a person's life. Is it possible, that we can become tired and weary spiritually as well? Is it possible that we can be weak and heavy laden spiritually? Is it possible that in our spiritual walk that we become faint? I believe we can become this way. I believe that we can be clicking away and then realize that something is different. We can realize at that moment that we are less than our best. Can this happen to us on our own spiritual journey? Again, I do believe it can. So how does it happen and what do we do to make sure that it does not become commonplace?

First of all, being spiritually exhausted comes from trying to find and please God in our own resources. We become weak and tired spiritually when our search for truth by our own efforts becomes wrapped up in human works or human wisdom. Such efforts include trying to earn salvation or achieve God's standard of living by our own human effort. This individual attempt to arrive at divine truth without God is like dragging around a 200 pound sack strapped to your ankle. Working our way to God and His presence is burdensome and it will wear us down. Fainting from a self-centered, works-centered life will be the result. We will become weary and heavy laden. We will faint. However, there is a remedy. There is a way to find God and to know Him without passing out from spiritual fatigue. There is spiritual rest in life. This is found in a person. His name is Jesus. Jesus tells us in Matthew 11:28-30 "Come to Me, all who are weary and heavy-laden, and I will give you rest. Take My yoke upon you and learn from Me, for I am gentle and humble in heart, and you will find rest for your souls. For My yoke is easy and My burden is light." Did you see this? His yoke is easy and His burden is light.

Walking with the Lord is a joy not a task. Having fellowship with Jesus is not a chore, it is delight. Abiding day by day speaking to Him, learning of Him is not wearisome, but refreshing, rejuvenating, invigorating, life-giving, a privilege, an honor, restful and enduring. So how do we avoid spiritual weakness and spiritual exhaustion? We come to Jesus. Once we are with Jesus, we rest in Him. We rest in Him and we abide in Him. We wait on Him for in so doing we will find the strength that we need to live this life we have been so privileged to receive.

Isaiah 40:31 says it wonderfully. "But those who wait on the Lord, shall renew their strength; they shall mount up with wings like eagles, they shall run and not be weary, they shall walk and not faint."

If you want to run in your spiritual life and not get tired, if you want to walk with Christ and not faint, then wait on the Lord. Don't force it. Don't worry about it. Don't work it to death. Just come to Him and He will give you rest. Wait on Him and in His timing you will find what you need in life. May we all find the rest that we need physically as well as the all-important rest and strength in our walk with our loving Lord.

Scripture reading: Matthew 5:16

Draw near to God and He will draw near to you.

Never Full

I enjoy all kinds of movies. I enjoy watching suspense thrillers, action types, and drama movies based on real events. I am looking forward to seeing a movie named '42' which is out now. Though I don't always get out to the theaters, when I do go and if I have chosen well, I usually have a great time watching it. In 2004 a movie came out that was a lot of fun to watch. It was called, *Pirates of the Caribbean - The Curse of the Black Pearl*. It had a combination of humor, suspense and just plain pirate fun. One of the scenes in the movie has always stuck with me however. To me it is very intriguing when you first watch it. The conversation takes place in the captain's quarters on the Black Pearl pirate ship. It is a conversation between Captain Barbossa and Elizabeth Turner (though not her real last name). The conversation is foundational to the movie in that it sets the stage for why these pirates were still on the hunt for Aztec gold.

Picking up in the discussion in the captain's quarters Barbossa says " Aye, that's exactly what I thought when we were first told the tale. Find it, we did. There be the chest. Inside be the gold. And we took em all. We spent em and traded em and frittered em away on drink and food and pleasurable company. The more we gave em away, the more we came to realize the drink would not satisfy, food turned to ash in our mouths, and all the pleasurable company in the world could not slake our lust. We are cursed men, Miss Turner. Compelled by greed, we were, but now we are consumed by it. There is one way we can end our curse. All the scattered pieces of the Aztec gold must be restored and the blood repaid. Thanks to ye, we have the final piece."

What a terrible situation Barbossa and his crew were in. They would eat and drink but nothing would satisfy. Food turned to ash in their mouths and all the company in the world would not curtail their compelling desire for more. Nothing would satisfy. What all of their shipmates reveled in, bragged about and sought after turned against them. Before this curse I am sure that it was a given amongst the crew that obtaining gold, spending it on food, drink, pleasurable company and whatever else they laid their eyes on was the thing to do. It was the hunt that they all pursued without even questioning the merits of their actions. They had been chasing after things, which in the end, found that it never did satisfy. It only left them empty with a continual lust for more. The problem was that until the curse was broken, they would never be satisfied, never full.

This is very common in our world isn't it? We desire something and then once we get it we want more. Why? Because the things we often chase after do not satisfy. They never will. What we often pursue in life is not meant to satisfy. We just think it is. We are not alone. Multi-millionaire John D. Rockefeller was once asked "How much is enough money?" He replied "Just a little bit more." You see, even for a man that could buy anything he wanted, there is never enough. Some have called this principle of increasing desire and decreasing satisfaction, a form of the law of diminishing returns. The more you want and desire, the more you are unsatisfied once you do get it. So what do we do? How are we supposed to look at things in life? Aren't we supposed to pursue our dreams? Aren't we supposed to go after goals, objectives, a better life for ourselves and our families? Let's go to the author of it all and see what he has to say about it.

First of all, I feel that there is a big difference between going after things and flat out being consumed and in love with things. For example, if one is consumed with making money, you will not be satisfied. Ecclesiastes says in 5:10 "Whoever loves money never has money enough; whoever loves wealth is never satisfied with his income." In other words, the good Lord does not want us to be so overwhelmed with things that we covet them more than anything else. If we do, then we will forfeit the perspective on life which He asks us to have. Hebrews 13:5 says it best. "Let your conduct be without covetousness; be content with what you have. For He Himself has said, "I will never leave you nor forsake you." Contentment while pursuing the dreams which the Lord has put on your heart is the viewpoint we all need. We should never not do our best but we must always examine our motives for why we are going after the things that we are setting our sites on. A man once said "When we focus on material things, our having will never catch up with our wanting."

As you go after your goals in life, know this. We will only be fully, completely and consistently satisfied when we walk with the living God. Only He can truly and perfectly satisfy our souls as we hunt in the areas of our callings. As we pursue our dreams in life, let us realize what things can truly satisfy. If we don't realize this tendency to misdirect our focus, then we may find that our pursuits may only be ashes in our mouth. We will never be full. Keep dreaming, keep working hard, keep pursuing excellence and keep doing your very best each and every day. However, do all of this as you are drawing close to the Lord. He loves you and knows that in His presence is true joy.

Scripture reading: Psalm 16:11

Draw near to God and He will draw near to you.

Never Out of Range

Several nights back I was the keynote speaker for the WFU Archery Club's Award Banquet. They had club members, parents and grandparents from as far away as Minnesota take part in the celebration. The club gave away the most improved, most valuable and rookie of the year awards as well as several other unique recognitions. In only its 3rd year, they have increased membership from 10 to over 60 dues paying members. It was truly an honor to be asked to speak at the club's awards presentation.

Throughout the evening, the club spoke on many of its accomplishments. They spoke on the first annual Hunger Games tournament, their movement from a club to the club/varsity level, and then the team and individual accomplishments at the national archery championships this spring. Throughout the evening, the club's motto was printed everywhere. It was on the ceremony program, on their team shirts and on many slides during the numerous still and video shots of the club. Though the saying does not match reality, it does give an air of confidence which every archer must carry into competition if he or she desires to be successful. Though not exactly accurate, it does communicate a standard which has pushed this club to being one of the best new clubs at Wake Forest. The motto is this: Wake Forest Archery: "Never Out of Range."

In the sport of Olympic archery, targets are placed at only one distance. Since the 1972 Olympics this distance has remained the same for men's and women's divisions as well as individual and team matches. This distance is 70 meters. Every target placed at 70 meters is within range of these highly skilled and poised athletes. However, if you were to move the targets to 170 meters, they would reach the target but accuracy would be greatly diminished. If the target were to be placed at 770 yards, the archers would be totally out of range. So, if one of these club archers were asked to nock an arrow and pull a 200 pound recurve bow to the cheek and then release, the arrow would fall woefully short of the intended target if placed at 770 yards. The current world record for farthest shot ever made is just shy of 500 meters or around 546 yards. Therefore any attempt at a target in the neighborhood of 770 yards is out of range.

However, there is an area in life that no matter how far you step it off, you are never out of range. You may walk to 800 yards, you may go across town, across the state, even across the country and you will continue to never be out of range. Whether you climb the peak of Everest or dive to the bottom of the Mariana Trench in the Pacific Ocean, you are still never from this reach. What can have such a reach? How can anything possibly have such a reach? The Lord God almighty is the One, the only One who can reach us whenever and wherever we are. He is "Never out of Range."

Psalm 139 speaks of this. "O Lord, you have searched me and know me. You know my sitting down and my rising up; you understand my thought afar off. You comprehend my path and my lying down, and are acquainted with all my ways. For there is not a word on my tongue, but behold O Lord, you know it altogether....Where can I go from Your Spirit? Or where can I flee from Your presence? If I ascend into heaven, You are there; If I make my bed in hell, behold you are there. If I take the wings of the morning, and dwell in the uttermost parts of the sea, even there Your hand shall lead me, and Your right hand shall hold me."

We are never out of the Lord's reach. We are never in a location, in a situation, in a hardship, or in a victory that the Lord God Almighty is not there as well. So what do we do with this truth? What difference does this make in our lives? First of all, it should comfort us to know that we always have a friend and master who is there with us. Whether it is early in the morning or late in the evening, He is shoulder to shoulder with us no matter what situation we find ourselves in. There is never a time in life when we are alone. The Lord Jesus Christ is right there with us. So with this truth we also can be confident. We can be confident that the creator of the universe is pulling for us to be everything that He created us to be. There are no secrets that we can hide from Him. He sees it all. He knows our thoughts. He knows when we lie down and when we rise up. He even knows what we are thinking and eventually saying. In spite of all of that, He still loves us and wants to have a friendship with us. He sees it all. He is never out of range.

God is right there with you. Speak with Him often. Be totally transparent. He knows you better than you know yourself. He loves you and wants to be there for you not only this day but for every day of your life. Some day you will meet Him face to face. Until then, start getting to know Him more and more. He is the source of everything good, everything lasting and everything meaningful. He is never out of range.

Scripture reading: Matthew 10:30

Draw near to God and He will draw near to you.

Out of the Garage, Made New

It is always fun to get something new. Whether it is a new pair of shoes, a new phone or a new sports jacket, it feels good to have something that has never been worn, never been tried out or never been put to regular use. However, getting something new is usually pretty rare. It doesn't happen very often because getting something fresh off the shelf or fresh out of the box usually costs quite a bit of money. Most of us do not have the ability to buy something new whenever we want so the occasion is special when it does happen. Because it is so costly, many times we have to wait a long period time for the chance to get something new.

In my garage I have many things that were once new. I have old shoes, baseball bats, exercise equipment, two televisions and bags of old clothing. Some day real soon I am going to back my truck up against the garage door and load all of it into the bed of the truck. I will either take the items to the Rescue Mission, to Goodwill and if it is in really bad shape I will go to the Forsyth County Landfill and pitch it into a large dumpster. Once out of the dumpster, it will eventually be emptied onto the landfill and covered with dirt.

When things move past their usefulness, items are discarded and considered unimportant. When our possessions are stained with dirt, dented on the sides, and well worn, cracked and spent, then they are considered worthless and of no value. All of these items which have lost all of their luster, their crisp functionality and their smell of newness will end up in garages like mine. At that point they will wait for the day when they are finally taken away to the place where all similar objects are discarded, waiting to be covered over with soil.

There are many people in our world who feel like they are sitting in a garage as well. Some folks only a few doors down, across the street or on the other side of town, consider themselves worthless and of no value. Through choices that they have made and the subsequent scars that oftentimes accompany such decisions, many men and women feel like they are in a bag, feeling unimportant, unworthy, useless, only to be discarded at the next bulky item pickup time. Such people feel like they are muddy, stained permanently, broken on the inside and past any hope of being useful and of value. They feel like a ton of bricks have been placed on their backs from life's heavy load. They work hard to put up a good cover but deep down inside they feel like one of those items in my garage. They feel useless, spent, and incapable of impact. Many feel only worthy to be cast away far from life's stage.

The bible talks of individuals who feel this way. The bible, which is the Lord's words to us, mentions situations when people are bent, cracked or are spent. God's message to us discusses those who feel this way. And then, after such sentiment is shared, the Lord has a response. After the garage like situation is communicated, the Lord through His inspired word, gives His perspective. It is a perspective which we must never forget. It is a perspective which every person, in every town, in every neighborhood, in every room of every home, who is struggling with life must hear. It is a word from the Lord God Himself. It is a word to those who feel like they have missed their chance. It is a word which I heard many years ago and it has changed my life, totally and forever.

In the gospel of Matthew, the Lord takes items which are normally thrown away and He says that He will not discard them. Using the imagery of a reed (like a clarinet reed) vital to the playing of music and a candle wick essential for the giving of light to a room, the Lord says He will not break nor snuff them out. "A bruised reed He will not break, and a smoldering wick he will not snuff out." What is He saying? He is saying that no matter what state that you are in, whether you are a broken reed which used to make music or a candle wick which used to give light, He will no wise cast you out. You are precious. You are valuable. You are needed. You have a purpose. You have value. You can make a difference. You are worth God's only Son dying for. How can this be? Some of you may say, "You don't know what I have done. You don't know what I have been involved with." The Lord says that He will not put you out. He has a purpose for your life. "How do you know this?" You may be asking. "Don't you know that I am weak, I have a load of care, a load of wrongdoing and a load of sin in my life."

Jesus says, "Come to Me, all you who labor and are heavy laden, and I will give you rest. Take my yoke upon you and learn of Me, for I am gentle and lowly in heart, and you will find rest for your souls. For my yoke is easy and My burden is light."

You may still be thinking "Yes, I want to come to Him. However, will I ever get out of the garage? Will there ever be a second chance for me? Will I ever have a chance to feel like a new pair of shoes, a new car or a new jacket? Will I ever, can I ever, be made new again? Is it possible, to start this whole life over again? Is it possible to be a new person totally washed from the dirt and put back together again with a new life to live?" The answer to all of these questions is a resounding Yes, an enthusiastic Yes, a blasting and echoing, Yes. Yes. Yes. A new life is possible. A new start is within our grasp. A new hope, a new joy, a new purpose and a new perspective is all within our reach.

The Lord calls us in Isaiah 1:18 "Come now, and let us reason together." says the Lord, "Though your sins are like scarlet, they shall be white as snow; though they are red like crimson, they shall be as wool." We can be new creations. II Corinthians 5:17 says "Therefore, if anyone is in Christ, he is a new creation; old things have passed away; behold, all things have become new."

So how do we have our sins washed away? How do we get to be in Christ and therefore become a new creation? It is only a genuine prayer away. It is only an open, honest and sincere prayer away. The prayer which begins such life transformation is a prayer acknowledging Jesus Christ's death on the cross and resurrection from the dead. It is a prayer believing that since Jesus rose again, that you can have forgiveness of sins and experience His forever presence in your life. It is a prayer receiving Jesus Christ to be your Lord and savior. If you want this new life; if you want to have all things made new; if you want your sins washed away, if you want to receive Jesus, then say this prayer even where you are right now. "Dear Jesus, thank you for dying on the cross for my sins. I accept you and receive you into my life this very moment. Come into my life and make me into the person that you want me to be. In Jesus name amen."

If you prayed that prayer, you are a child of God. If you prayed that prayer, you are a new creation poised to be molded day by day into the person the Lord wants you to be. If you have prayed that prayer, your sins are washed away and you are new. If you prayed that prayer for the very first time, let someone know who also is a Christian. He or she will then encourage you and hopefully point you to a bible study or church where you can grow as a brother/sister in Christ.

New shoes are great but nothing can compare to the new life which only Jesus Christ can provide. Thanks for your partnership in this great adventure. Great days await us. Let's stay the course and encourage one another along the way.

Scripture reading: John 1:12, II Corinthians 5:17, I John 5:13

Draw near to God and He will draw near to you.

Seemingly Safe, Unbearably Hot

I did something the other day in the kitchen which I have not done for years. I should have known better than to do what I did but I stumbled into doing it anyway. After I did this foolish act, I shook my head in disbelief. I learned this lesson years ago. Why was I learning it all over again? Why now in midlife. Nevertheless, with my carelessness, I was reminded that even though I am much older, I can still make mistakes just like I did when I was in my early years. The lesson I was supposed to have learned years earlier left me yesterday. It left for just a second but that was all it took to send me across the kitchen in disbelief.

The frying pan was on the stove fresh out of the oven holding my dinner. The pan was bubbling in its prepared sauces. I grabbed the scalding hot pan which was just taken out of the oven, wrapping my entire hand around the handle. Once my hand was tightly gripped onto the handle, a metal handle with 100% heat conducting capacity, the sudden firing of nerve endings began their immediate journey. Within milliseconds, through the pathways of strategically placed nerves in my hand, the sense of severe pain registered in the key areas of my brain. I immediately let go, stepped back and said "ouch." I shook my hand, and gazed into the palm of my hand looking for immediate blisters to form. I got burned from grabbing a hot pan. Even a day later, my hand was still tender. I cannot remember the last time that I grabbed something that hot. I felt like a 2 year old who had never known the danger of a 400 degree metal pan on exposed skin.

Looking back on the incident, I have tried to figure out why I would have done something so absent of common sense. Thinking further about what had happened, it finally dawned on me the reason why I reached and grabbed something so hot. When I pulled the pan out of the oven to begin with, I had forgotten about the temperature of the pan. I used hot pads to get the pan out of the oven but I forgot from which the pan had come. Upon returning to finishing the meal, my gaze went to the pan but it looked perfectly normal, perfectly safe, perfectly cool, perfectly benign, and perfectly acceptable to touch and to move. The problem was that in reality the pan was piping hot. I thought it was one way and it was another. I thought that the pan was cool but it was hot. I thought it would be safe to touch but it hurt me. I was tricked. It was red hot and I did not recognize it. I forgot about things that are in the oven with the temperature on high. I was not cautious. I went head long into a situation and got burned.

There are lots of pans in your world sitting out there every day calling out for your attention. From the outside they look safe, they look cool, they look benign, they look totally attractive and acceptable. However, once you wrap your hand around it and pick it up, you get burned. What you thought was one way, suddenly turned out to be the totally opposite. What am I speaking of here? What pans am I referring to which look safe on the outside but inside are dangerous? What things in life could potentially send one yelping across a room, looking at the damage to oneself and feeling pain for extended periods of time? What can look perfectly normal only to be hot and not perform any good in one's life? Answers: We get into trouble when we are: 1. tempted by our own desires, 2. when what we think we are looking at is safe and it is in fact the enemy and 3. when we forget our marching orders.

1. James 1:13-17 "Let no one say when he is tempted, "I am tempted by God" for God cannot be tempted by evil, nor does He Himself tempt anyone. But each one is tempted when he is drawn away by his own desires and enticed. Then, when desire has conceived, it gives birth to sin; and sin, when it is full-grown, brings forth death. Do not be deceived (tricked), my beloved brethren. Every good gift and every perfect gift is from above, and comes down from the Father of lights, with whom there is no variation or shadow of turning."
2. II Corinthians 11:14 "And no wonder! For Satan himself masquerades (disguises himself) as an angel of light." In other words, he devises schemes which appear seemingly safe but are unbearably hot.
3. Matthew 10:16 "Behold, I send you out as sheep in the midst of wolves. Therefore be as wise as serpents and innocent as doves." - The Marching orders - choose wisely.

There are lots of ways to get burned by various pans in the world. Because space is short I will only touch on one pan which if we are not wise, can burn us pretty bad. There are many others but this one has destroyed many relationships and many families over time. Though only focusing on one side of a front burner situation, it does take two individuals to do the damage which can separate the best of friends.

Proverbs 5:3-6 says "For the lips of an immoral woman drip honey, and her mouth is smoother than oil; but in the end she is bitter as wormwood, sharp as a two-edged sword. Her feet go down to death, her steps lay hold of hell. Lest you ponder her path of life; - Her ways are unstable; you do not know them."

And in similar fashion in Proverbs 7:21-27 "With her enticing speech she caused him to yield, with her flattering lips she seduced him. Immediately he went after her, as an ox goes to the slaughter or as a fool to the correction of the stocks, till an arrow struck his liver. As a bird hastens to the snare, he did not know it would cost his life. Now, therefore, listen to me, my children; pay attention to the words of my mouth; Do not let your heart turn aside to her ways, do not stray into her paths; for she has cast down many wounded, and all who were slain by her were strong men."

Men and women, when you walk into the various kitchens in your life this day and the coming days, recognize which pans are hot and which ones are safe. If you are not sure, consult the temperature gauge of life, the word of God. Don't ignore the prompting of the Holy Spirit when He says not to touch it. Life is meant to be lived in peace and joy. "Trust in the Lord with all of your heart and lean not on your own understanding. Acknowledge the Lord in all of your ways and He will make your paths straight." Prov. 3:5, 6.

I will see you in the kitchen. Choose wisely and pray for each other to do the same.

Scripture reading: Matthew 10:16

Draw near to God and He will draw near to you.

Trust

In just about every setting in life, I do not believe that there is any more important word than trust. In my employment world I need to trust those who I work for, those I work with and those who work for me. In family life, wives need to trust their husbands, husbands need to trust their wives, the children need to trust their parents and the parents need to trust their children. Trust is foundational to the smooth operation of just about any relationship or organization that you can think of. In sports, trust is the fulcrum by which all things balance in the quest for excellence and victory. For example, the pitcher must trust the catcher to make the right pitch calls. In football, the quarterback must trust his offensive coordinator to call in the right play at the right time. In basketball, when a man breaks free and you must leave your man to stop the uncontested layup, you trust that another teammate will come to your aid and take your man. Whether one is governing others, serving others, confronting others or even competing against others, life is full and meaningful when trust is foundational.

What do we trust people for? We trust that the truth is being told. We trust that intentions are genuine. We trust that the other person is doing things the right way. We trust that all are looking out for each other. We trust that people's best interests are being protected. We trust that folks are being treated in the most fair, consistent and honest way possible. When all of the opportunities to interact are positive, encouraging, helpful and good, then trust is established and strong. However, when trust is not in the air, as we all know, everything gets pushed out of balance.

When an embarrassing situation in your life is shared with others, trust can be broken. When a story shared in confidence is retold without permission, trust can be broken. When privileges which are given are taken advantage of and transgressed, trust is broken. When words which are spoken do not align with the truth, trust is broken. When a possession is abused, misused or thoughtlessly cared for, trust is broken. When responsibilities are neglected, ignored or are never attended to, trust is broken.

As I type this list of situations which break trust, my mind goes back to times when I have not been trustworthy. When pondering the times when others break my trust, I must think back to times when I have been less than trustworthy myself. In fact, as I think of trust and broken trust, I can honestly say that there have been times when I have broken a trust. I have spoken ill of someone behind their back. I have not taken care of the things which I was entrusted with. I have not been the person that I know I needed to be. I, at times, should not have been trusted. I did not deserve to be trusted. My motives were not right. My actions were not right. My behaviors were not right. I should not have been trusted because I was not responsible with the things entrusted to me. However, there is a person who always can be trusted.

Maybe your life is a little different. Maybe you have always been trustworthy and have been around people who have been trustworthy. Maybe you have always done the right things and had friends who have done the right things for you every time. Maybe your life has been surrounded by people whose motives, actions and behaviors have been at the highest level 100% of the time. However, I believe that this has not been the case for most of us. I believe that we have been untrustworthy at times and others around us have been untrustworthy as well.

In spite of our experiences where trust might have been broken, in spite of the pain which came with it, in spite of our pasts, there is a person whose trustworthiness can change it all. There is a person who can be trusted when others have not been trustworthy. When all is known about you, there is a person who will never leave us nor forsake us when others fly the coop. There is a person who we can be totally transparent and honest with when others are not available. There is a person who can be trusted no matter what we have done, where we have been or how far we have gone down the wrong path. There is a person who knows us better than we know ourselves and still loves us even while we were yet rebellious. This person is Jesus Christ. He can be trusted and He can be trusted in.

So, has someone broken your trust? Jesus is there. Has someone been less than a friend? Jesus is there. Has a situation or life circumstance let you down? Jesus is there. Since trust is so important to life, who or what have you been trusting in? Have you been trusting in your money? It could go. Have you been trusting in your good looks? They could and will go. Have you been trusting in your intelligence? You will not be as mentally sharp one day. Have you been trusting in your status, privilege or family line? Times and families change.

The Holy Scriptures speak often of trusting in God. Why? Because He can be trusted. " I will trust in your unfailing love" Psalm 13:5, "I lift up my soul, in you I trust" Psalm 25:2, "But I will trust in you, O Lord " Psalm 31:4, "Trust in Him at all times, O people" Psalms 62:8 , "For I trust in your word" Psalm 119:42 " , Trust in the Lord with all of your heart" Proverbs 3:5, "The Lord is good. A stronghold in the day of trouble; And He knows those who trust in Him" Nahum 1:7.

You may be blessed with some friends who are rock solid, who can be trusted. Such friends are like gold. However, some of you may not have had individuals in your life who can be trustworthy. Such individuals are out there. They can be found. It sometimes just takes time. However, whether you have trustworthy friends or not, Jesus Christ is there. He can and will fill your needs. Go to Him today. Share your concerns with Him. Express your fears. Tell Him your dreams. Jesus can be trusted fully. In fact, you can trust Jesus in every area of your life. Trust Him today and then go and be a trustworthy friend to another. Be a trustworthy person. Be someone who will protect a relationship. Be the person who another can be open and honest with. Our Lord can be trusted. We can follow His lead and strive to be trusted as well. Trust in the Lord and be trustworthy.

Scripture reading: Nahum 1:7 "The Lord is good. A stronghold in the day of trouble; And He knows those who trust in Him."

Draw near to God and He will draw near to you.

He is There and He is Not Silent

What makes humanity different from all other life forms? What makes you and me different from the tree, from the deer, from the ant, from the fish? We are different from all other creatures in that we have the ability to communicate with language, with words. We do not retrace our steps back home by our sense of smell. We do not make various calls into the sky. We do not growl, grunt or howl when deciding to go forward or retreat. No, we use language. We use clear verbalized words symbolizing our thoughts, our feelings, our emotions, our intentions as well as our directives all through the spoken and written word.

True communication happens when one has an idea. He or she then puts the idea into a series of words. This idea with its targeted intent is then perfectly transferred into the mind of the hearer. In other words, if a relationship is going to occur or grow, one party must voice a message to the ears and mind of another. Yes, communication can take place non-verbally with pictures, gestures, sounds, and the like but specific directive words are absent. Yes, creation does speak to us through a beautiful sunset, a roaring tornado or a warm breeze on a beach but it is only general in nature. Specific, pointed, focused communication is missing in the sunset. Verbalizing words with meaning is the essence of true communication.

In Genesis 1:26 God says "Let us make man in our image." Man is made in the image of God. God before He created man communicated fully in the Trinity. There was perfect continual communication between the Father, the Son and the Holy Spirit. God is a triune communicative being. Man is an image bearer of God so man is like God in a way. We are like God in that we are able to communicate just like He has always been able to communicate. Therefore, if we are communicative beings and communicating to each other; if we are made in the image of God being different from every other creature; wouldn't it be reasonable that between God and those created in His image there would be communication? Yes, I believe it is perfectly reasonable.

Many times I have talked of prayer. I have talked of keeping company with God, being open and honest with Him, being candid with our thoughts, our disappointments and making requests to God. However, in every relationship that is truly a relationship, there is two-way communication. If I have a relationship with God, I should be able to talk to God (prayer) and He should be able to talk to me. God is not silent. He has spoken. True relationship is possible.

When I fly home to Alaska to visit my dad, I usually walk into the living room and sit down next to my dad. I oftentimes just begin talking. I talk of my day, my trip north, my hopes, my disappointments, my struggles and my victories. My dad in return does not sit in his chair motionless, expressionless and staring out into the front yard. If that occurred, I would say that there is really no relationship. I would say that it is one way if a relationship at all. You see a relationship, a true relationship, involves words coming from me and words coming from my dad. I talk and then he talks. He talks and then I listen. I talk again and then he talks. You see, how can I ever know the wisdom of my 84 year old dad unless he speaks to me?

How can we know the wisdom of the God of all creation unless He speaks to us? Well, He has spoken. He is not silent. He has told His story. He has listed His wishes, His instructions and He has even warned us of the possible pitfalls and tendencies of mankind. He has told us of the purpose of life, revealed to us the secret power of life, promised the peace of life and even explained how we can be pardoned from all of our rebellious sin. He has explained the Son from which all of life's true joy proceeds. He has even told us what the future will look like.

I want to hear from God. I want to sit at His feet and hear His wisdom. I want to hear truth. I want to be warned of the lies. I want to speak with dad, our heavenly dad, our Heavenly Father and let Him speak wisdom into my life. His words to us can and will make a difference in our lives and all those in the world who will listen. Let's hear some of His reminders of His words to us.

Psalm 119:105 "Thy word is a lamp to my feet and a light to my path." II Timothy 3:16 "All Scripture is given by inspiration of God and is profitable for doctrine, for reproof, for correction, for instruction in righteousness that the man of God may be complete, thoroughly equipped for every good work." Matthew 4:4 "Man shall not live by bread alone but by every word that proceeds from the mouth of God."

Hebrews 4:12 "For the word of God is living and powerful, and sharper than any two-edged sword, piercing even to the division of soul and spirit, and of joints and marrow, and is a discerner of the thoughts and intents of the heart." Colossians 3:16 "Let the word of Christ dwell in you richly in all wisdom, teaching and admonishing one another in psalms and hymns and spiritual songs, singing with grace in your hearts to the Lord." Psalms 119:11 "How can a young man keep his way pure? By taking heed according to Your word." Romans 10:17 "So then faith comes by hearing, and hearing by the word of God."

When the battle of the work day slows down, store up God's word in your heart. Set your mind on things above. Crave the pure spiritual milk of the word. Watch out for the medicine men wanting to lure you away from truth. Stand firm. As II Timothy 2:15 says "Be diligent to present yourself approved to God, a worker who does not need to be ashamed, rightly dividing the word of truth.

You can do it. You can see life how it is supposed to be seen. You can be able to call out to falsehood saying "that is bogus, that is a lie, that is not life; that is counterfeit." You can do it if you find the truth. It can be found. God is not silent. He has spoken in His words to us. I am pulling for you and am convinced that God is able to bring this good work which He has started in you to completion. Don't give up. Don't chase after what the world claims is the answers. Pursue God. Pursue His truth.

If you do, I am convinced that you will live a life that is full, meaningful and abundant. John 10:10 Jesus speaking, "I came that they may have life and have it abundantly."

Continue to be salt and light in a world looking for answers.

Draw near to God and He will draw near to you.

The River Narrows

Today, many of you might be thinking that life is good. With the week being almost over, a holiday weekend fast approaching and summer vacation just around the corner, life appears to be good. A Boston based company came up with the 'Life is Good' slogan many years ago and it is now everywhere. They created a stick figure man named Jake and now has a dog image named Rocket. They are screened and embroidered on gear ranging from backpacks to water bottles. Life is good but you know what? Everything changes when you find out what is out there. Everything changes when you get a glimpse of the other side of life.

One of my first summers as a commercial salmon fisherman in Alaska, I fished on a boat called the Bounty. One day before a big salmon opening, the skipper posed a question to us deckhands, "Guys, what you think? Should we stay in the narrows of the river, the river narrows, or go out to deeper water?" At the time I was what you call a beginner or a greenhorn with no real experience in such decisions. The other deckhand was about the same with only a few more years of experience. So after looking at each other for a few seconds, we turned to the skipper and said," deep water. We have been there before and that is best." The skipper said "Alright then, let's kick her in gear and get going."

Once at the fishing spot that we had chosen and the fishing time becoming official, we threw the buoy out the back of the boat. We dropped a long sockeye salmon gillnet off the stern going out to around two football fields in length. Once the net was all the way out, we tied it off and began peering at the net hoping that we picked a good spot. After a couple minutes, we saw a splash. A sockeye salmon had hit the net. After a couple more minutes another one hit. We were catching fish one by one. After about 30 minutes, we probably had 30 - seven pound sockeye salmon in the net. John and I were happy. We were catching fish and with our 10% percentage at $1/pound, we were making some money, not much but some. We were doing just fine. What we had going was good. It was acceptable to us. We were satisfied. Life was good.

After a few more minutes, our skipper thought that he should call one of his fisherman friends to see how they were doing. He got on the VHF and called out "Seawolf, Seawolf, this is the Bounty come in." There was no answer. He called again "Seawolf, Seawolf, this is Bounty, come in." He called again and still no response. Beginning to get a little worried because of the silence, he decided to call land. He knew that his friend's wife always had the radio on so he decided to call her. She would know the status of the Seawolf.

The skipper called land and got ahold of the wife of his friend who was out fishing. "Hello", our captain inquired, "We have been trying to get ahold of Don and there has been no answer for quite some time. Do you have any news?" After a long pause, she finally said, "Oh yes, yes. We have news. Don is fine. He just has not been able to answer any calls. He has been too busy." We all perked up at that moment as our skipper inquired, "What do you mean too busy?" "Oh, I'm sorry," she continued. "Don has not been able to answer any calls because his nets are all sunk to the bottom of the river. You see he set his net in the river narrows. He set his net in the river narrows and the fish were so thick that they sunk his net. The corkline is still underwater and the entire net is sunk. It is taking him a long time to get all of those salmon out of the net. All of the fish holds are getting full and it looks like he will have to put another 10-12,000 pounds on the deck of the boat. It looks like he will have over 22,000 pounds of sockeye salmon. That is around 3,000 fish. Isn't that great Jack? His nets are sunk! Oh, and one more thing" she continued. "Several of the boats who were in contact with each other all went up into the river narrows and their nets are sunk as well. Talk to you soon." I will never forget that moment for the rest of my life.

We had no idea. We were happy with what we were catching and their nets were sunk. We had 30 fish thinking that we were doing well. They had 3000. You see, once you find out what is out there, it changes everything. In similar fashion, once you find out about what life can be like with the Lord, everything changes as well.

Guess what? People everywhere have gone up into the spiritual river narrows of a close life with the Lord and they have sunk their nets. In fact, many are sinking their nets all around us right now. Their spiritual nets are plugged. They have loaded all of their fish holes and have so much in spiritual abundance that it is spilling over onto the deck. How do I know? I have been on the VHF radio and have heard about it. More than that I have seen their nets. I have seen their lives. I know, catching 30 salmon is good but catching 3000 is better. You may think that life with a partial interest in God is good but you have no idea. Life is best when the Lord is in your life totally. You can have more. You can have much more.

Over the years, many people have gone up into the River Narrows and have sunk their nets. They have sunk their nets at home, in the community, in all dimensions of life, including the physical, mental, social, and the all important walk with our Lord. So as a Stephen Curtis Chapman once wrote, "You're wading in a puddle when you should be swimming in the ocean, playing Gameboy in the middle of the Grand Canyon, eating candy sitting at a gourmet feast, Wake Up, Wake up and see the Glory." Where are you heading in life? Are you heading to deep water or toward the River Narrows?

Many of you are settling for deep water when the Lord has so much more in store for you. Many of you are settling for a lifestyle which is staying with what is comfortable and it does not include God. You might be thinking that life is good. The problem is that you have no idea that there is so much more in life, so much more that you could be experiencing. This abundance, which may be foreign to you at the present, is only found in a personal relationship with the living God. This River Narrows is beyond, way beyond, what some of you may be settling for at this moment. Don't take the bait and run out to the familiar and safe deep water. Turn to Jesus and allow Him to fill your life with all that the Almighty Father can provide.

Jesus said in John 10:10 " I have come that they might have life and have it abundantly." Jesus came so we could travel into the River Narrows. Jesus came so we could receive all of the spiritual blessings available to us from the heavenly places. Jesus came so we would not settle for just good in deep water, but for that which will fill our nets, fill our boats and fill our lives with His presence, His joy, His meaning and His abundant life.

Are you ready to make a direction change? Are you ready to follow Jesus into the River Narrows? Are you tired of trying to do it your way and are ready to do it your Maker's way? If you are ready, I promise you that you will never, ever regret the change in direction. I will be praying that whoever is reading this today will turn towards the River Narrows. It is the only place where life is truly lived. Steer away from deep water and go where

Jesus is. Will you come? Jesus is waiting. He wants to bless your life. He is willing. Will you go? I will be looking for you.

Scripture: Ephesians 3:20, Joshua 1:8, Psalms 1:1-3

Draw near to God and He will draw near to you.

Work Until It Is Finished

Many times my work day, especially over a weekend, starts pretty early and finishes kind of late. For example, one Saturday a few weeks back, I woke up taking on the first on the task list at 5:45am and finally finished the day at 7:45pm. Several things had to get done that day so that is why the day took so long. For one thing, I had to open up and prepare the gymnasium for an event scheduled on campus. A second major task involved a dead tree that needed attention in the back yard. The winterized chainsaw had to get cranked up for some needed cutting. Another item on the list involved my son being invited to a paintball party as well as birthday party. I was the taxi service. Lastly, we needed an exterior motion sensing light installed and some yard weed killing concentrate, so errands to Lowes Home Improvement were on the list.

Several things had to be done, so like many of you when you get a chance, I worked until it was finished. Starting in the yard, I clipped dead limbs off several trees and shrubs adding to the ever-growing brush pile. In between a few short errands, I was able to pick my son up from paintball just in time to take him home for a quick shower and then off to another party. After getting him to the party, I had a couple minutes so I mixed five gallons of the weed killer to apply it to both the front yard and the hill in the back yard. After that, with food supplies running low and Debbie out of town for the evening, I had to do some shopping for groceries. At 8:05pm everything appeared to be finished so I finally sat down for some dinner. However that didn't last too long. Our dog Sadie had been in the house most of the day and she needed to be taken for a walk. When it finally became dark outside and no more exterior work could be done, I finally called it a day. My mind was a little tired, my legs were slightly wobbly and my arms were dragging the wagon. It was a good hard day of work. Stuff had to be done and I had to keep going until it was finished.

Why is it that work never seems to get totally done? Why is it that when we clip one dead limb we look over and there are 20 other ones needing to be taken down, sawed up and stacked onto the burn pile as well? Why is it that the more that we do, the more we find out that we have only scratched the surface on the task list? There is always something to do. It is never finished. I can work on my studies. I can work on the yard. I can work on my reading. I can work on getting caught up with emails. I can work out. Work. Work. It is never over. It is never finished. There is a job to be done and I have to be diligent to get it done. However, in spite of all of the sweat, the sore muscles and hours in study and mental preparation, why is it that work is still such a good thing? What is it about work that is so positive, so rewarding, so necessary for our well-being and the world in which we live? I believe work is good because it is something that our Lord has asked us to do.

I Thessalonians 4:11 "...that you aspire to lead a quiet life, to mind your own business, and to work with your own hands, as we commanded you." The book of Proverbs has much to say about work as well. Chapter 10:4 "He who has a slack hand becomes poor, but the hand of the diligent (hard worker) makes rich." Chapter 12:24 "The hand of the diligent will rule, but the lazy man will be put to forced labor." Chapter 13:4 "The soul of the lazy man desires, and has nothing; but the soul of the diligent shall be made rich." And Chapter 21:5 "The plans of the diligent (the hard worker) lead surely to plenty, but those of everyone who is hasty to poverty." II Thessalonians 3:10 says "If anyone will not work, neither shall he eat."

Work is therefore good. Working for those things which are good, is even better. In fact, we were created to do good works. Ephesians 2:10 says "For we are God's workmanship, created in Christ Jesus for good works, which God prepared beforehand that we should walk in them." Working with all of our being and giving God the credit is an attractive testimony before a watching world. Matthew 5:16 challenges us to "Let your light so shine before men, that they may see your good works and glorify your Father in heaven." However, there is a disclaimer which God requires when we put our back into any project or task. Colossians 3:23 reminds us of the motive which the Lord desires us to have whenever we put our hands to something. "And whatever you do, work heartily, as to the Lord and not to men."

The Lord has set the example of work. He showed us in the beginning when He created the heavens and the earth. And then, over 2000 years ago, He showed us His work of salvation when He went to the cross. At creation, the Lord's most prized work was man and woman who He created in His image. At the cross, Jesus did a great work as well, a work which has eternal implications for you and for me. At the cross, Jesus just before He died, He uttered a phrase which signaled the end of His greatest work. He said "It is finished." He is now sitting at the right hand of the Father poised to return at the time of His choosing. The Lord's work of paying the penalty for our sins is done. It is finished.

Jesus is the only one ever born whose sole purpose and primary work was to die. He had a job to do. He had a great work to do. He did not stop until it was finished. The false accusations didn't stop Him. His friends abandoning Him didn't stop Him. The crown of thorns and the scourging didn't stop Him. The realization that He would bear the sins of the entire world did not stop Him. The knowledge of the fact that the Heavenly Father would turn away and be separated from Him for the first time in all time did not stop Him. Jesus had a work to do. He saw it through. He fulfilled the task that He was born to do. Now, He can say that His work on the cross is over. It is finished. Thanks be to God.

We all have a job to do as well. Jesus Christ, God in the flesh, has ascended to heaven. We now are His hands and His feet. We now are His workmanship created for works that He has planned for us. Are you willing to do the work that He has for you? Are you willing to seek and find out what He wants you to do? Are you willing to pray and ask Him to reveal the things He wants you to be doing each and every day? Are you willing to do the job that you were born in Christ to do? If you are willing, then you will be on your way to the great adventure, an adventure of a lifetime designed in heaven just for you.

Wait on Him. Listen to His whispers. Read His directions. Pray for His guidance. Seek counsel from Godly folks. Then someday, after a lifetime of following His will for your life, you will hear His words to you. "Well done, good and faithful servant. Come and enter into your rest."

He will then say to you that it is finished. The work is done. It is now all joy, all pleasure, all satisfaction and all fulfillment in the company of your fellow brothers and sisters in Christ. Keep working hard.

Keep giving it all you have. Do it for the Lord and not for men and their recognition for we are God's fellow workers and will receive our reward if we do not grow weary in well doing. You have what it takes.

Scripture reading: Ecclesiastes 9:10,

 I Corinthians 10:13,

Colossians 3:23

Draw near to God and He will draw near to you.

Words or Silence?

A couple weeks ago I attended a retirement celebration for a friend of mine. The room was packed with individuals showing their appreciation. The room was abuzz with professionals and students awaiting the opportunity to recognize a man of renowned and unselfish service. This gentleman served our community in various capacities for almost 37 years. This is an amazing feat when you think of today's average job tenure (2.8 yrs). While I listened to the four main speakers, I was humbled by their words and stories of this man's gift to his place of employment.

Two colleagues spoke, a subordinate and then finally his superior, the one who he works for. All of them had very similar things to say. All of them spoke of his countless hours of service, his genuine love for those in his care and his wise counsel to those he mentored. He was described as a thinker, a teacher, and a leader of change. As I listened to the words being spoken, I gazed across the room and began to think of something myself. My thoughts were stirred as I saw the smiles on the faces, heard the sounds of their applause and felt the love in their hearts for a man who had given so much to them for so long. As I turned to walk out of this retirement celebration, I asked myself about the day which will eventually have to occur for all of us. I asked myself; will there be words or silence?

As I walked out of the room and out of the building, I thought ahead to my own last day on the job. What would it be like when it is my last day? What kind of descriptors will be used when they speak of my life, my words, my actions and my time spent with others? What kind of stories will be told of the time spent with those needing my support? Will there be words or will there be silence? Will the room be jam packed like it was that day at my friends? Or, will no one even show? Will the room be filled with lives that have been encouraged, challenged or touched in some positive way? Or, since my life was only spent on myself, will no one even take time to stop by my going away celebration? Will there be colleagues, subordinates and then ultimately my superior all saying the same thing about me revealing a life of faithful consistency? Or, will the stories of my life be like the waves of the sea, up and down and all around? Will my life and work be talked about and appreciated? Or, will there be silence because no one could remember a time that I went out of my way to help anyone in their time of need? Will there be verbal and possibly tangible gestures of their love for me? Or, will there only be an announcement in the company newsletter marking my time there? Will the speakers recite poems that described my life as being an impactful and successful leader, teacher and friend? Or, will no poem, no story, no testimonial at all being uttered or written in any journal, speech or article describing my time there? Will the speeches spoken remind the hearers that the one before them was trustworthy and kind, speaking the truth in love, no matter what the obstacle? Or, will there just be silence? Silence indicating that I was not trusted, was not kind and thoughtful, did not speak the truth to those needing truth, and always compromised when times got tough? When I walked out of that celebration, I thought of these things wondering what will be the setting and words delivered on my final day. Will there be words or silence?

When you walk across the stage saying goodbye to your place of employment maybe in a few weeks, maybe in a year or maybe in a few years, what will be said of you? What will be the legacy that you will leave behind? If there will be a time when people could come to the microphone on that retirement day, what will be said of you? What words, phrases and stories will they tell to describe the impact that you had in their life? Will there be silence? Will they struggle to find words and examples of unselfish living because there were none? Or, will they recite time after time, day after day examples of when you showed them what an honest person, a trustworthy person, a hardworking person, a faithful person, a Christian, looks like? Will they talk of periods in their life when you pulled out of what you were doing just to stop in and say hello, just to take them out to lunch, just to tell them that you were there if they needed you, just to say that you would be praying for them? Will there be words or will there be silence?

There is an old hymn that goes like this, "When we all get to heaven what a day of rejoicing it will be, when we all see Jesus, we'll sing and shout the victory." Someday our tenure on this earth will be done. Someday our day jobs on this earth will be over. Some day my fellow partners in the gospel, we will be done with our place of employment, done with school, done with sports seasons, done with certifications and internships, trainings and management tracts. Someday my fellow image bearers of God, our lives will be over and our life will be brought before the microphone. In that day, we will listen and hear all about the opportunities which we all had in front of us each day. Stories of our interactions with colleagues may be told. Stories about interactions with subordinates may be told. However, the most important story will be the one told about our interaction with our superior, the ultimate superior, Jesus Christ. Jesus Christ will step up to the microphone and announce to those in the room all of the accomplishments which gave glory to Him and which ones that did not. Will there be lots of folks in that room that day who received your special touch in their lives? Or, will the room be empty? Will Jesus have lots of things to say about the works that you did for Him, for His children and for mankind? Or, will He be silent? Will His only words speak of His grace which was sufficient, which paid your way to paradise but there be no mention of crowns, no discussion of rewards and then no mention of a special job or task which the Lord will have you do in glory? As someone once said, you will be in the parade (in heaven) but because of the lack of service to the Lord you will be so far back that you cannot hear the band. Will there be words from the microphone or silence?

So what do you do with the time that you have? Make the most of every opportunity. Look for opportunities to give credit to the Lord. Look for ways to be the hands and feet of Jesus. Look for tasks which cause people's eyes to turn to Jesus. In whatever you do, work heartily for the Lord and not men. In whatever you do, know that there is not only a loving God watching and pulling for you, but there is a watching world looking for someone who lives out what they claim. The world wants so desperately to say "There walks a man or woman who lived what he said, lived his faith, gave much away, and made a difference in the lives of many." Words or silence? What will it be? I hope that there will be a long line to the microphone that day for you. I hope that you have invested so much in others during your time here on earth that each person speaking will be held to a five page limit. Start building today. It's not too late. You can do it. What will it be? Words or silence?

Scripture reading: Romans 14:12, Luke 12:48

Draw near to God and He will draw near to you.

Teachers We Know, Teachers We Are

The last Club Sports Union meeting of the year at Wake Forest University was a lot of fun. Numerous awards were handed out, lots of jokes were tried and of course at least one story was told. Since it was the last meeting of the year, the room was at capacity with just about every seat taken. The outgoing president of the Club Sports Union spoke, the co-president shared some thoughts and then I had some parting words for the officers. Even though there is not enough room here to share all of the things that I covered that night, I would like to revisit the story that I told the group. The story was about teaching and the kinds of teachers that we have had in our lives. Teachers can come from schools, churches and work places but they also can come from family. The story that I told was about a little boy who had a teacher. The teacher was his grandpa.

Many years ago, there was a grandpa who knew and demonstrated the principle of teaching. He wanted to teach his little grandson about all kinds of things in life. He would talk of everyday life, of church, of family, but then he would sit the boy down and tell him about his favorite pastime. He would tell him about his favorite sport. He would tell the little boy about the sport of baseball. He would tell him of the greats from the past like Sandy Kofax, Satchel Page, Mickey Mantle, and Stan Musial. However, he would not just tell him about it, he would teach him, demonstrate the game to him and finally give him opportunities to play the game as well.

In the front yard of the little boy's house, the grandpa would pitch the ball to the little guy all afternoon just about every day. The grandpa would pitch the ball and the little boy would hit the ball heading off for first base as fast as he could run. As the ball would hit and travel way out into the yard, the grandpa would turn and walk toward where the baseball finally settled. Once getting to the ball, he would pick it up and walk back towards the pitching mound. While the grandpa was walking, the little boy would run around the bases tagging first, second, third and then home just about the time that the grandpa would arrive back at the pitching mound. Over and over this routine would take place, summer after summer, year after year, between this little boy and his grandpa. The little boy got into elementary school and he continued to hit the ball and throw the ball. In junior high he continued but the grandpa would only teach and watch for the little boy was getting too big to pitch to. Each year as the little boy got better in the game of baseball, the grandpa/the teacher got older and older in age. Nevertheless the grandpa still taught the little boy as he grew.

In high school, the little boy continued to hit the ball and throw the ball with continual encouragement from the grandpa. Then one day, in his senior year in high school, the little boy came running into the house saying, "Grandpa, grandpa I am going to college to play baseball. Arizona State University just called and I am going to play Division I baseball." The grandpa said "fine my grandson." But to the grandpa this was kind of foreign for he did not know much about college baseball, he only knew of professional baseball.

Well, the little boy went off to college and the teacher, the grandpa, would hear about the grandson each weekend. "Your grandson hit a home run today," he would hear. Or "Your grandson struck out today." But with each year the granddad, the teacher, continued to get older and older. Each year, as the grandpa got older this little boy who was now a grown man in college continued to get better, faster and stronger in the game of baseball. Then, at the beginning of summer, on June 10, 1983 the day of the Major League baseball draft, this little boy with his grandpa just a room away got a phone call. The voice on the other line said, "Hello, this is the Philadelphia Phillies, you have been drafted in the 14th round. We would like you to come and play for us in our farm system with plans of playing in the big leagues very soon." So the little boy ran to the other room and told his teacher, his grandpa, about the call. "Should I go grandpa?" he asked. "Of course you should go." replied the grandpa. So the little boy went off to play for the Philadelphia Phillies. However he did not know that once he left that he would no longer see his teacher, his grandpa, ever again.

Several weeks later, in Bend, Oregon playing single A baseball, the little boy was handed a telegram in the clubhouse. It was from his mother. It was about his grandpa, his teacher. It went something like this "Max, your granddaddy has gone on to be with the Lord today. Do not worry, for he is in good hands. Continue to play like you used to play all those years ago. Continue to hit the ball and run those bases like you did in the front yard just like you did with grandpa. He would have wanted it that way. Love, Mom."

Do you have a teacher in your life like that? I had one. He made a difference in my life. I will never forget him. They are out there. You just have to open your eyes. If you have had a teacher who has pitched to you for quite some time, are you willing to be the teacher now yourself? Some person is out there. They are waiting for you. Are you willing to give of yourself and walk after the ball while others run the bases?

230

Are you still teachable? Will you listen and learn knowing that those moments with those teachers do not last forever? Join in and teach about the things that matter. Join in and be teachable. Like the memories which I have with my grandpa and will never forget, go make some memories for another.

How will people know the truth unless someone tells them? How will people know which way to go in life unless someone points the way? How will someone know what life is supposed to be about unless someone explains it to them/teaches them? Like my granddad who told me and showed me the game of baseball, we have the answers to the major questions of life. The answers come in the form of a person. It is the one who was, who is, God in the flesh. The answer to the questions of life is Jesus Christ. John 14:6 tells it best. Jesus speaking: "I am the way, the truth and the life, no one comes to the father but by me." Go tell it. Go live it. Go believe it. Go show it. Go. When you do, you are following the wishes of the one who gave it all for us.

May you be a teacher in someone's life this coming day and every day. I know a little boy who had a grandpa who taught him much. May you be that kind of influence in someone else's life. They are waiting. Just go. There are teachers we know and teachers we are.

Scripture reading: Matthew 4:19, Colossians 3:16, Romans 10:17

Draw near to God and He will draw near to you.

Runaway Ramp

A few days ago my wife, my youngest son and I drove up to the mountains near the Blue Ridge Parkway for the afternoon. We ate some lunch, saw the new climbing wall at Appalachian State University and did a little outlet shopping before heading back down the mountain. Once we decided to head for home, we knew it would be a steep drop in elevation. Sure enough, our ears starting popping as we passed the last scenic pull out. While heading down this steep Highway 421, I saw many warning signs. Sign after sign warned truckers to gear down and stay to the right. The speed limit was allowed to reach the maximum for our small car but for the truckers they were repeatedly asked to gear down and check their breaks before driving down the steep decline.

Driving up the mountain earlier in the day, my mind was elsewhere and I did not notice something that I became aware of on our downward descent. I noticed something that I hoped no one would ever have to use. I saw a wide road attached to the main road some 40 feet or so wide and close to 300-400 feet in length. It had 10 or so huge piles of sand piled high one right after the other from the beginning of this adjacent road to the end. I knew exactly what it was for. For a moment, I visualized the plight of a driver who may have to use it someday. As you know, I am speaking of a runaway truck ramp. Placed strategically half way down the steepest grade on the mountainside, this runaway ramp was there for any trucker who has lost his breaks. This ramp is for truckers who may have lost control and may be concerned about their life, their cargo or everyone else on the road with them. As I viewed this runaway ramp, I remembered seeing dozens and dozens of them over the

232

years. All of them were strategically placed like this one on mountain roads all across our country.

Though not an expert, I am sure that the storyline leading up to the need to use one of these runaway ramps is pretty much the same. First of all, the truck in question may not have checked the brakes or the brakes were already in poor condition. Second, the truck driver may have hit the downgrade at a speed beyond the breaking capacity. Most likely he or she would be still in a high gear continuing to propel the truck at an ever increasing speed down the mountainside. Thirdly, I believe that the most trucks in this predicament usually have a lot of cargo. Therefore, with the weight of the truck, plus poor brakes and excessive speed, most trucks would be on a course beyond what any regular driver could endure. In addition to the aforementioned, some trucks are prepared but the drivers have approached the mountainside with overconfidence and little concern.

Many in this latter situation involving overconfidence and lack of concern may have found themselves in this mindset because of the following: They might have been distracted by drifting thoughts, a deep conversation, an interesting radio station or just the surrounding scenery. All of these contributing factors coming together at the top of a mountain road can create a perfect storm of trouble causing many unsuspecting truckers to experience a ride that they would not normally choose. If they fail to be watchful, they will need a runaway ramp like one that we saw that day. If they are not careful, they will need a way to get off the road. They will need a way to slow down in order to protect the truck and its contents. They will need some kind of help in order to stop this dangerous momentum downward. Finally, they will need a runaway ramp to help them stop what they are doing and to help them start all over again. Driving by these runaway ramps that day I was thankful for those who took the time to build them. To those who are in trouble, having a runaway ramp could save their life.

We all need runaway ramps in our lives. At times we need getting off points thus giving us opportunities to start all over again. We may have entered a time in our life when we have lost our capacity to brake. We may have approached a hill when we were going way to fast not keeping our speed under control. Even this day, for some of us we may be heading down a steep grade and we are just carrying way too much payload. We may have too much going on in our lives which is putting excessive weight on our life's truck frame. Or, like the everyday truckers, we may have hit a roadway propelling us downward and we are just not paying attention. We are watching and listening to other things that are taking our minds off our truck and the road.

I do not know where you are in your life. Some of you may be thinking that you have good brakes and that you know how to gear down and stop when you need to. Others of you may be saying to yourself that you are not going too fast and are not recklessly speeding. Still others may be saying that your load is light and that you are not distracted one little bit. However, there may be one reading this who may need this reminder. There may be one or more of you who may feel that your brakes are out, the speed is getting way out of control, the cargo hole is too weighty and the distractions are continuously pulling you away from your focus on life. There is an off-ramp for you. There is a runaway ramp just for you. It is there to slow you down, help you to reduce your speed, remove unnecessary weight in the cargo area and give you clear vision to see life more fully. This ramp is a person. This saving road is God in the flesh. This stopping point giving you the opportunity to change your life is the Lord Jesus Christ. He is there for you when the road in life is out of control. He is there for you when you need a fresh start. He is there for you to change your situation and make you into the person which He created you to be.

II Corinthians 5:17 tells us of the results of pulling off the road and coming to Jesus, the runaway ramp. "Therefore, if anyone is in Christ, he is a new creation, old things have passed away, behold, all things have become new." And Matthew 11:28 "Come to Me (Jesus speaking), all you who labor and are heavy laden, and I will give you rest. Take my yoke upon you and learn from Me, for I am gentle and lowly in heart, and you will find rest for your souls." And I John 5:12 "He who has the Son has life, he who does not have the Son of God does not have life." And finally, Acts 3:19 " Repent (get off the road) then, and turn to God so that your sins may be wiped out, that times of refreshing may come from the Lord."

It is never too late to pull off the road. Remember that Jesus will always be there for you. He will never leave you nor forsake you. He is the way, the truth and the life. He is the runaway ramp not only for those speeding downward but for every one of us. Every one of us, no matter what our situation, whether in the nicest set of trucker wheels or ones without brakes, all of us desperately need the Lord Jesus Christ. For there is no other name under heaven by which one can be saved, there is no other name under heaven who can guide us safely down the mountainsides of life..

Pull over today if you need to. He is there. He is our ever present help. If you are doing well, share this truth with someone else today. In so doing you may save someone from a bad, bad crash.

Scripture reading: I Peter 4:8, James 5:16

Draw near to God and He will draw near to you.

Valentine's Day Hearts

Their packages arrived just in time for Valentine's Day. Though one of my sons got his a little late, both of my daughters received what I give all of my children every year on Valentine's Day. Emily and Abbey went to their post office boxes and found a box addressed to them. Inside was their traditional box of chocolates with a Valentine's Day card from their mother and me.

Earlier during the week of Valentines, before the snow hit, I went by the post office and picked up a box which could hold the large heart shaped box of chocolates. I could have gotten a rectangle box of chocolates which would have been more conducive to shipping but that would not have worked. The box had to be heart shaped. As you know, the shape of Valentine's Day is the heart. Though I am sure that they would have liked the chocolates anyway, my daughters needed to know that the chocolates were wrapped in a heart. The heart is the symbol of love, of appreciation and of care. The heart also at the seat of emotions and is foundational to every relationship which is cherished.

Even my wife got in on the fun. She surprised us all with red velvet pancakes topped with white icing and heart shaped sprinkles. As shown in this loving gesture, the heart once again played a key role with its representation of love, of appreciation and of care. The heart is what maintains marriages, sustains families, bonds friendships and grows service to the needy. All of these vital connections find fulfillment in a heart that is in the right place. However, there is another connection much more vital than any marriage, any family, any friendship or service. There is another relationship which has the heart as its

237

foundation. This relationship which focuses on the heart is our relationship with our loving Lord. He wants our heart. God's holy word explains it best.

Deuteronomy 4:29 "…you will find Him if you seek Him with all your heart…"

Deuteronomy 6:5 "You shall love the Lord your God with all your heart, with all your soul and with all your strength."

Deuteronomy 11:13 "…to love the Lord your God and serve Him with all your heart and with all your soul."

Proverbs 3:5 "Trust in the Lord with all your heart, and lean not on your own understanding."

Psalms 51:17 "The sacrifices of God are a broken spirit, a broken and contrite heart. These, O God, You will not despise."

I Samuel 16:7 "For the Lord does not see as man sees, for man looks at the outward appearance, but the Lord looks at the heart."

Proverbs 23:19 "Listen my son, and be wise, and keep your heart on the right path."

So on this Valentine's Day, will you trust in the Lord with all of your heart? Will you seek Him with all of your heart? Will you follow Him with all of your heart? Will you obey Him with all of your heart? You can count on Him. He will guide you. He can comfort you. He will be your fortress and your strength if you let Him. He knows you and will never ever leave you. He knows your secrets. He knows your fears and loves you regardless, more than we could ever imagine. He wants to give you a heart that is upright, fearless, undivided, pure, steadfast, secure and wise. Will you abide in His love even this day?

With every Valentine's Day the symbol of love is the heart. Whether it is a heart shaped box full of chocolates, heart shaped sprinkles on pancakes or a small red, white or pink candy with "Be my Valentine" printed on it in red letters, the symbol is the heart. Valentine's Day symbols are the heart.

However, there is another symbol which seems to be a better descriptor of our Heavenly Father's love for us. It is a symbol which every time I see it I am truly reminded of His love for me. No, it is not a heart. It is a symbol which communicates obedience, sacrifice and endless love. The symbol is the cross.

Romans 5:8 says it best. "But God demonstrates His own love toward us, in that while we were yet sinners, Christ died for us."

On the next Valentine's Day, as you express your love to family and friends, be reminded of our Lord's love for us. As you send a card, make a phone call or send a text, please recall the greatest demonstration of love that the world has ever known. Remember that God came down from heaven and gave His life so that we should not perish but would have everlasting life. May that thought be the filter of our life's dreams, our life's relationships and our life's service. He wants all of our heart. Will you give it to Him this day? Will you follow Him this day? If you do, I promise you that you will never regret it.

If you let Him, He can give you immeasurably more all that we could ever ask or imagine.

Scripture reading: Matthew 6:21

Draw near to the Lord God almighty and He will draw near to you.

One Umbrella, One Life

One week ago yesterday 8-10,000 relatives and friends watched and waited for the one they came to see to walk across the stage at the 2013 Wake Forest University's graduation ceremony. Once all deserving participants received their diplomas, they returned to their seats waiting for the signal to cheerfully launch their caps into the air. There was a slight problem which was building while the graduation celebration was taking place however. There was a large band of thunderclouds making there way towards campus. These rain ready clouds would find their mark just as the ceremony was completed.

When the rain clouds finally decided to unleash its contents, it came like flood waters from the sky. Graduates, family members and relatives seemed to weather the rain for a few minutes but after the rain did not let up they dashed from the open and sought cover wherever they could find it. Some made it into buildings. Others got to their cars. Many had rain protection such as an umbrella or rain jackets. Those who got caught in the weather and did not have umbrellas or rain jackets were drenched from head to toe.

I was prepared when the rains came. I had watched the weather forecast and had brought an umbrella just in case we got hit by a gullywasher. When the rains came I was dry, safe and comfortable. It was an interesting time when the first wave of family and friends came running by looking for shelter. While under the umbrella I watched quietly as the masses were exposed to the torrential rains. They were caught in the rain with no protection from the elements. I had one umbrella surrounded by a sea of humanity most of whom were caught with no protection. What was I supposed to do about this situation I thought to myself? What could I do? What should I do?

As I walked towards my car, I passed a gentleman covering his head with a soggy graduation program. Soon afterward several others crossed in front of me with a similar fate. I walked on feeling no rain, no cold and no discomfort. I passed one more person and then a thought came to my mind. I thought, "Max, there is nothing you can do to help these people. There are just too many. All of these have made wrong choices concerning the weather. They are just feeling the consequences." I continued to walk towards my car and got ready to pass yet another group of unfortunate parents. All of these caught in the rain had a focused, serious and frustrated look on their faces as they could not wait to get to shelter. Then something came to my mind which impacted my walk from that point on.

As I looked at the overwhelming number of people needing shelter, I made a decision. Instead of hunkering down under my own umbrella and gloating in my situation and the misfortune of others, I decided to reach out. The very next person appeared to be a mother of a graduate. She was also caught in the downpour unprepared. I thought to myself, "No, I cannot help them all but I can help this one." I came up next to her, put the umbrella over her head and said, "Maam, I know this may be a little late but would you mind a little help?" Though reluctant at first, she said yes and received my help. I walked with this mom until our paths took a turn at the parking lot. She said "thank you" and we parted ways.

What was the lesson that I learned that day? I believe part of it was this: I cannot help the entire world but I can make a difference for one. I cannot impact the entire world in a positive way each day but there could be one individual who could benefit from my umbrella overhead. I may not be able to feed the whole world but I could feed one. I may not be able to provide clothing for every child in the cold but I could give clothes to one. I may not be able to share the good news of Jesus Christ with every person in the world but I can share Him with those who are in my sphere of contact.

Who in your world have you lent your umbrella to this day? Who have you spent time with lately thus sheltering them from possible isolation and aloneness? Who have you shared your gifts with so as to bring protection? Who seems to be stuck in the rain in your life? Who seems to be walking and always seems to be caught in the rain of misfortune? No, we cannot help everyone. However, we can help one life. We can help the one who is walking in front of us hurting and getting drenched from life's rain.

Will you take the opportunity this day? Will you share what you have gained and what you know in order to meet the needs of this one today? I know it is safe and dry underneath that umbrella of yours but gifts are not here to be put under a bushel. Gifts, talents and possessions are here to benefit the lives of others as well as ourselves. Step up beside someone and offer your umbrella. You will never regret that you did. Many are rushing around looking for shelter but many are looking in all the wrong places. You have the good news of Jesus Christ. Share it and show it.

James says in Chapter 1 verse 27 says "Religion that God our Father accepts as pure and faultless is this: to look after orphans and widows in their distress and to keep oneself from being polluted by the world." And I John 3: 17, 18 "If anyone has material possessions and sees his brother in need but has no pity on him, how can the love of God be in him? Dear children, let us not love with words or tongue but with actions and in truth." And Jesus speaking in Matthew 28:19 "Therefore go and make disciples of all nations, baptizing them in the name of the Father and of the Son and of the Holy Spirit, and teaching them to obey everything I have commanded you. And surely I am with you always, to the very end of the age."

Yes we may only have one umbrella. But to that one person who you give cover to, it can literally change their life. So give someone a phone call today and provide relationship cover. Ask someone to lunch tomorrow who cannot repay you and provide food cover. And if the opportunity presents itself, invite a friend to church, to a bible study or to a get together which will have faithful Christians in attendance. You have one umbrella; share it with one life today. Jesus shared His life with us. We can share ours with others as well.

Scripture readings: Hebrews 13:16, I Timothy 6:18

Draw near to God and He will draw near to you.

Two Rescues

For my birthday my wife took me to the famous Daniel Boone restaurant in Boone, NC. The home style cooking and atmosphere was a lot of fun. As you are probably well aware, Daniel Boone made quite an impact on westward expansion in our country. Specifically, he made the Wilderness Trail passable impacting close to 300,000 settlers. This feat allowed many to move through the Cumberland Gap towards the ever growing western frontier. Many towns and counties have been named after Daniel Boone because of his can-do spirit. He symbolized what it was to be an early pioneer, an explorer and a frontiersman. Daniel Boone accomplished much to catapult himself into extensive fame during that time. Of all the things which he did to etch his name in history, there was one which seems to stand about the rest. It involved a daring rescue. This rescues involved Daniel Boone rescuing his daughter and two other girls from a Cherokee/Shawnee raiding party which had carried them away.

Jemima Boone and two other young girls were paddling in a canoe just outside of the fort at Boonesborough, Kentucky when an Indian raiding party attacked. The raiders carried them off north intending to cross the Ohio River out of the reach of the unsuspecting settlers. Daniel Boone immediately organized a rescue party and overtook the raiders two days later as the Indians were preparing breakfast. Boone and others shot and killed one of the Indians and scattered the others thus spoiling the kidnap attempt. Years later this exploit of Daniel Boone would reach the pen of a fictional writer by the name of James Fenimore Cooper. He wrote of a similar kidnapping and eventual rescue in his 1826 book entitled, "The Last of the Mohicans", one of my now all-time favorites.

Rescues always seem to draw wide scale acclaim. Within the last few years there have been some wonderful rescues accomplished by men and women showing skill, determination and inexhaustible hope. In August of 2010, 33 Chilean miners were trapped over one mile below the surface in the San Jose copper-gold mine. They were trapped underground for over 33 days before being unbelievably rescued. In 2009, Captain Chelsey Sullenberger safely guided a jet down onto the Hudson River after a flock of geese stalled both engines. All 155 passengers and crew were safely rescued. On October 14, 1987 a baby girl by the name of Jessica McClure fell into a well and was trapped 22 feet down. After two days, they rescued 'baby Jessica' after drilling through solid rock. Then, in 1970 when I was a young boy, news came across the airways of an explosion on the lunar bound Apollo 13. The explosion knocked out much of the electrical system leaving the astronauts 200,000 miles above earth with limited power and slowly loosing heat. Six days later the Apollo 13 safely landed in the Pacific Ocean allowing the men to be rescued. All of these rescues will never be forgotten in my mind and the minds of countless others.

However, there is one other rescue that exceeds all of these wonderful documented rescues. There is a rescue attempt and completion which went beyond the return of a baby, passengers, miners or even astronauts suspended in outer space. There has been a rescue documented in history which if chosen to acknowledge and accept, will surpass any act of bravery, any act of determination, any act of love and compassion that the world has ever known. There has been a rescue personally experienced by literally millions through the years. It is the most notable, most important and most impactful rescue which the world will ever see. Without this rescue, the world and countless lives would not be where they are and who they are today. This rescue was not performed by a team of drillers, nor from a team of experts at NASA or a ship on the Hudson. This rescue was performed by one person and one person alone. It was a rescue which could only be done by this one person. He and He alone did what only He could do. He came to be a rescuer. This person who is my rescuer, your rescuer and the rescuer of the entire world, is God who became flesh and dwelt among us. This rescuer is the Lord Jesus Christ.

Jesus came to seek and to save those who were/are lost in their trappings of sin. Jesus came to rescue us from the slavery of sin which we are born into and under the penalty of. Jesus Christ is the only one who can rescue us from this dark hole of sin that we were or are currently in. Jesus Christ came to rescue us. Jesus came to rescue us from our sins which if not paid for will keep us in a spiritual mineshaft, a spiritually dark water well or a spiritual lostness in space. Jesus is the only rescuer of these sins which everyone must come to terms with. Questions: Has Jesus rescued you? Have you put your faith and trust in Him so He can carry you out of life's trappings and wash your sins away? Jesus is knocking on the mineshaft. Will you call up to Him? Jesus is at the base of your downed plane. Will you jump in the boat with Him? Jesus is knocking on the door to your heart. Will you let Him in? He wants to rescue you. He wants to save you from the penalty and burden of your sin. Will you let Him? If you do let Him rescue you, it will be the best thing that you will ever do. If you let Jesus rescue you, it will be one of those rescues which will literally be talked about in heaven for all of time. All of us who have allowed Jesus to rescue us will be rejoicing knowing that you have joined those who have also made it to the surface. It is not too late. Grab on. We are all waiting for you and for everyone else who is still trapped. What a rescuer we have in Jesus. Thank Him today. Thank Him every day. Thank Him and then tell others of the rescue that they can and must enjoy before their air in life runs out.

Scripture reading: John 3:16, Romans 8:1-2

Draw near to God and He will draw near to you.

Pull the Tarps

As one of the NCAA Baseball site representatives in Columbia, South Carolina, we had to suspend the game last night between Liberty University and the University of South Carolina. Lightning struck within an eight mile distance so we pulled the players off the field and sent 8,000 fans to shelter. Once we got the players to safety, the grounds crew went to work. They rolled out a long 25 foot tube three feet in diameter which was wrapped with a water proof tarp. They unrolled the tarp from the tube, spread the tarp out in the outfield and then with all possible hands on deck, they pulled the tarp into position. The grounds crew pulled the tarp directly over the entire infield area thus protecting the most critical part of the ball field. With this huge tarp in place, the home plate area was covered, the pitcher's mound was covered and the entire base path was covered. It was a beautiful thing to see. It was a perfect covering.

Without this tarp, we would have had a hard time trying to finish the tournament. Without this covering, the entire infield, the main playing area of a baseball game, would have been a soppy mud field. We could not have even considered suspending the game without this tarp. Most programs across the country do not have such a tarp wide enough and thick enough to cover their field. Most programs do not have the ability to lay it out even if they had one. These tarps are extremely expensive. Yet, even though they are costly and an unbelievable chore to put out, they are a life saver to a baseball game or tournament like this NCAA Regional Championship. Without the tarp at our disposal last night, we could not have hoped for a chance to finish the game today. Without this covering, the rain would have soaked and ruined the entire infield. Without this covering, the rain from the inclement weather would have destroyed any hope of playing the game of baseball as it is supposed to be played. This covering protected us last night and because of it there are wonderful possibilities today. I am so thankful for that tarp, for that covering. The rains came but because of the covering that we had, the field was like new.

As I looked out at the field last night with the heavy rains pounding the tarp, I thought of another covering which I have seen and experienced. As I gazed in amazement at the perfect covering protecting the game surface, I thought of another perfect covering exceeding even the one I was peering at. As I watched the rain beat down, I thought of another covering which has been put in place to protect us from the beating down of life. This covering not only protects us from the pounding rains of life, it actually rebuilds our entire field. The covering of which I speak is the covering of Jesus Christ. Jesus Christ is our covering. Jesus Christ is the tarp who wraps around our life protecting us from sin's dominion. Jesus Christ rebuilds the field and then unfolds His expansive love and watches over us during the sunny days and the stormy days of life. Jesus Christ is a covering because He has promised that He will never leave you nor forsake you. He will always be in place, covering you from ever being enslaved by sin again. Is it true that we will sin after Jesus forgives our sin and grants us eternal life? Yes, we will. However, because Jesus has died on the cross for our sins and rose again, sin no longer permeates my being. I am now a new creation. II Corinthians 5:17. I am now protected. I now have a covering, a covering who never leaves me, no matter what the weather of life.

Do you have the most important, most costly tarp covering for your life? Do you have the covering in place which will protect you during the storms of life? Has your playing field been rebuilt and the most sacrificial tarp ever given to mankind been put in place? Or, are you still exposed? Is your field of life still the same? If not, I challenge you to trust in Jesus Christ and have your field of life rebuilt. Then and only then will you be protected by the covering of Jesus Christ. Are you still the same field that you have always been? Is nothing different? Do those habits and a wayward lifestyle still rule your life? Trust in the Lord Jesus Christ today and then let Him cover your life. If you do, He will protect you. He will keep you. He will cover you and change you so that your field will be all that you were created to be.

Psalms 32:1"Blessed is he whose transgression is forgiven, whose sin is covered. "Psalms 85:2 "You have forgiven the iniquity of Your people; you have covered all their sin."

Is your life hid with Jesus Christ? If it is, then what about your friends, acquaintances, classmates, neighbors, fellow workers or family members? Are they covered? Are they protected? Remember, when life is over and every person, from every land, from every tribe, in every nation stands before a holy God, the only ones who will enter into their rest are the ones who have the tarp, the covering of Jesus Christ. Look out to the playing fields this week and see who has the tarp of life in place. If they do not, will you help? Will you lead them to the tube where the tarp is located? Share Him. Live Him. Be like Him in all that you think, say and do this week.

Scripture reading: Psalms 32:1, Psalms 85:2, Romans 4:7

Draw near to God and He will draw near to you

The Wrong Finish Line

I love to watch track and field meets. Just a few days ago, I was able to watch an invitational collegiate track meet at Wake Forest University. After watching the 100 meter dash and the pole vault warmup, I decided to focus my attention onto the women's 1500 meter run. Since I now enjoy middle distance running, I had to watch this one. 12 runners lined up to give it their best in hopes of qualifying for the finals the following day. After one lap of this grueling four lap race, it was pretty close. The group was packed together just about the entire time. In lap two, the competitors seemed to stretch out a little bit. Nevertheless, it was still anybody's race. On lap three, the pace quickened. All seemed to be positioning themselves for the much anticipated final lap. However, about half way through the third lap of this four lap race, something happened that I will never forget.

About halfway through lap number three a competitor from the back of the pack began her kick. She passed the 11th and 10th place runners and then proceeded to blow past the 9th, the 8th, 7th, 6th and 5th place runners as well. With about 100 yards to finish the third lap of a four lap race, she ran past the 4th, 3rd and 2nd place runners. With 50 yards to go in lap number three, she whizzed by the first place runner in a full sprint lunging to the front as she crossed what she thought was the finish line. As soon she finished lap number three, she stopped in exhaustion thinking that she had finished and subsequently winning the heat. Then something happened that will be forever etched in my mind.

Directly in front of this unsuspecting runner, the finish judge took a hammer and hit a metal bell. It was the bell signaling the last lap. There was still a full lap to go in the race. This young lady had sprinted to what she thought was the finish line only to find out that she still had an entire lap to go. Once the bell lap was rung, she became alerted to her predicament but now was exhausted.

At the start of the fourth lap, all of the remaining runners in the race poised themselves for the final push. All of the runners except the one who had run toward the wrong finish line. The young lady who thought she had made the finish line lifted up her downcast head and began to run again. She ran but now she was spent. Instead of having legs fresh enough to finish strong, she had nothing left.

At about a fourth of the way around the final lap, runner after runner began to catch the runner who ran towards the wrong finish line. After the 2nd and 3rd place runners cruised by, the 4th place runner caught her, then the 5th, then the 6th, 7th 8th and 9th. With about 100 yards to go, the 10th place runner finally caught her. At the true finish line, gasping for every breath she barely edged the last place runner.

I felt terrible for this young lady. It was really sad to see this young runner realize what she thought was the finish line was not the real finish line at all. She had planned everything only to find out that what she had planned was not the real thing. She had expended all of her energy thinking that she had done the race correctly only to find out that she had been wrong the entire time. As I turned to go, I could not help but think of the spiritual race that we are asked to run each and every day. There is an old song that speaks of this very thing. It is a song from a group called Truth. This song speaks about the same thing that I saw on the track that day. It talks of how people can think one way about life only to find out that they have been running towards the wrong finish line. This is what the song says,

"John has a new way of looking at life.
He's tired of his job, and his kids and his wife.
He said the secret to his success was leaving and finding himself.
Now he's someone to somebody else.
You say we've risen to a new age of truth.
You call it a spiritual Godly pursuit.

But I say, I say,
What if we've fallen to the bottom of a well, thinking we've risen to the top of a mountain?
What if we're knocking on the gates of hell, thinking we're heaven bound?
What if we spend our lives thinking of ourselves, when we should have been thinking of each other?
What if we reach up and touch the ground to find out we're living life upside down?"

What if we are indeed running towards a finish line and it is not the right one? What if we reach up and touch the ground to find out that we've been living life upside down? We cannot be tricked either by our own thoughts or someone else's on what the real finish line in life is. We cannot afford to run one lap let alone three laps of a four lap race only to find out that our planning and strategies have been that far off. God's Holy Word reminds us of this as well.

Matthew 24:4 "And Jesus answered and said to them: Take head that no one deceive you."

Lamentations 3:40 "Let us examine our ways and test them, and let us return to the Lord."

I Corinthians 3:18 "Let no one deceive himself. If anyone among you seems to be wise in this age, let him become a fool that he may become wise. For the wisdom of the world is foolishness with God."

Ephesians 5:6 "Let no one deceive you with empty words, for because of these things the wrath of God comes upon the sons of disobedience."

Stay the course set before you. Seek the Lord with all of your heart asking for guidance in this race called life. Go shoulder to shoulder with other brothers and sisters in the Lord who know where the real finish line is located. Look at the track of life through the lenses of God's holy word which will tell us when to pace ourselves and when to kick it in. May we all this coming week and year have our sights set on the prize at the end of the race as well. If we run the race well and finish at the correct finish line, we will hear Him say, "Well done, my good and faithful servant." May it be said to all of us on that day.

Run hard. Run with passion and run the right number of laps.

Draw near to God and He will draw near to you.

When Practice Ends

What is one thing which causes more anxiety in the lives of students than anything else? What one thing forces individuals to lock themselves into rooms, into the stacks of the library or into some out of the way hallway with only a table and a light? What is the one thing which gets the attention of parents, of coaches, of academic advisors and counseling staffs all across academia? What one event will determine whether there is a command of a topic, a skill or an entire genre in areas such as: history, physics, chemistry, foreign language, literature, management or economics? It is only a solitary event but it is also an indicator of the time spent much earlier in the week, in the month or in the year. This one thing which oftentimes totally captivates our minds and attention are tests.

It is the test which adjusts every schedule. It is the test which forces priorities to shift. It is the test which forces leisure time to have a conscience. It is the test which tells all whether attention was paid, whether diligence in study was applied, or whether comprehension of the subject matter was truly grasped. Every class, every team, every family, every business, every organization, every relationship, every person must experience a test.

For example, in a very common scenario involving a test, a room is set in a semi-circle. The atmosphere is somber and quiet. The professor walks into the room and every student's eyes are glued to the stack of exams in his hand. The professor walks by every desk and hands the student a four sheet stapled packet which has multiple questions written on the front and back. When all have received the exams he says, "You may begin." The test is on.

Another scenario takes place in the bottom of the 9th inning on a baseball diamond. The home team is down by one run with runners on second and third base. The coach walks to the mound hitting his right arm. He is asking for his closer, the 6 foot 5 inch, right handed flame thrower from Madison, Wisconsin. The batter steps into the batter's box, the pitcher toes the pitching rubber. The test is on.

How about the test situation when Frank didn't mean to say it but he did. He wasn't thinking when he revealed a cherished secret to another at a party this past Saturday night but he did. The lunch room was just about empty that day but who would have thought that his friend of three years would be there. A spot next to the window away from his friend was open. He finds the seat, sits down and pulls his drink to his mouth only to see his friend out of the corner of his eye. His friend had heard what he had said about him. He was offended and deeply hurt. His friend gained eye contact but had turned away. He saw Frank. Frank saw him. The test is on.

And finally, no one would know if you took it. No one would even notice. The company has lots of them and would not even skip a beat if it came up missing. The boss has left for the day. The room is empty. You have always felt that you needed one. You continue to think that it wouldn't hurt anyone. Then another thought comes to your mind. The object is not yours. The test is on.

Each and every day we will have similar choices to make. Standing before us each day will be the people, the projects, the causes, and the jobs which strain for our attention. As you walk to your car, as you go work or to the classroom, as you engage with the people who surround your life, you will have a choice to make. Should I think of the Lord in this endeavor? Should I look for His handiwork in this cause? Should I acknowledge His greatness to myself and others? Should I share what I know is true to a world who has no thoughts of God? The test is on once again.

I don't want to sensationalize and say that every day is a test but I do feel that to an extent it is. Each day we have a test set on our desk from the Master Teacher, the Lord Jesus Christ which will read: Question #1.Will you walk with Me today? #2. Will you follow My will for your life today? #3.Will you acknowledge me in your mind and before others today? It is just a three question test. It is a short test but oh how important. These are the test questions which are foundational to a purposeful, powerful, peaceful and perspective given life. How you answer these questions on this test will make all the difference in your life on a daily basis.

I will be praying for those who have read these words. I will be praying that you will excel in all of the subject matters which you will be tested on. However, during this week and the weeks to follow, I will be interested in this one other test which is written and delivered to us every day. Yes, I hope you pass this week's coming tests in the traditional classrooms with flying colors. However, I also hope and pray that you will be passing the test in the great classroom of life each and every day as well. Is your pencil in hand? Are you ready? Are you prepared? Do you want to ace it? The Lord Jesus Christ knows you can. He has given you everything that you need. It is now up to you. The test is on.

James 1:12 - "Blessed is the man who perseveres under trial, because when he has stood the test, he will receive the crown of life."

Psalm 26:2, "Test me, O Lord and try me, examine my heart and my mind."

Proverbs 27:21, "The crucible for silver and the furnace for gold, but man is tested by the praise he receives."

I Tim 3:10, "But let these also first be tested; then let them serve as deacons, being found blameless."

Draw near to God and He will draw near to you.

It is Finished

Five different seniors stopped by my office the other day. They came by to say goodbye. Graduation was just a few days away so they were making their rounds. We talked of many things. We talked about how fast everything seemed to happen. They felt like it was only yesterday when they were moving in as freshmen. Since all of them either worked for me or were leaders in one of our programs which I oversee, they also spoke of how much they appreciated the opportunity be a part of our world. However, there was one other thing that they all seemed to feel just after they walked in my door. They were amazed and sad but yet glad at the same time. They were glad that their goal was finally over. They were reflective yet really excited that their goal was accomplished, that it was finished.

Accomplishing what we set out to do in life is a great feeling. I like getting there every day. There is something about putting your mind to something, sticking to the plan and actually reaching the goal which you mapped out. We all need to be consistently setting goals. When we set goals, the setting of goals always seem to keep us moving forward. Goals necessitate planning, execution and finally evaluation. We all need to know and do our best when we have jobs to do. We all need to know these jobs and get after them each and every day. We all need to get to a point when we can say, "It is finished."

Whether you realized it or not, there are certain tasks in life which you were created to perform. There are certain jobs and projects which you and you alone are set up to accomplish. You have certain gifts, abilities and passions which no one else may have concerning a certain goal set before you. You may have unique time, talents or treasure which may set the stage for the achievement of a specific goals. Whether these ideas have come to your mind through academic study, from doing everyday life or from various interactions with people, we all need to have goals. Goals remind us of our place in this world. They help us to see the big picture. Goals give us direction, they give us a sense of purpose and they give us tangible measures to see if we are indeed doing the things we need to be doing.

Every tool has a purpose. Every device has a purpose. Every vessel has a purpose and every person has a purpose. God is the not only the master architect but He is also the master purpose giver and goal setter. Each person who comes into this world arrives with a certain package of gifts. Each person who arrives onto the scene of life arrives with the touch of the master's hand. Each person who has become a child of God, placing their faith and trust in the Lord Jesus, has work that only he or she is called to do. Ephesians 2:10 speaks of this: "For we are God's workmanship created in Christ Jesus for works which he prepared for us to do in advance." We all have jobs to do. We all have a service to perform. We all have a ministry to fulfill. We are created special by God to do something in this world which will not get done without our commitment to this goal. The Lord wants us to look over our goal when it is accomplished and say, "It is finished."

However, no complete discussion on goal setting could ever be complete unless we talk of the greatest goal ever accomplished in the history of mankind. No discussion of goal setting would be intellectually honest without bringing up the most recognized and pivotal completed goal in recorded history. Over 2000 years ago, Jesus of Nazareth came to earth with one primary goal to perform. He accomplished His goal. Jesus Christ came to die. In fact, Jesus is the only person who ever lived whose singular purpose after birth was to die. John the Baptist confirms this idea when he first laid his eyes on Jesus. He said, "Behold, the lamb of God who takes away the sins of the world." Jesus Christ came to this earth to be that sacrificial lamb. He was to take our sins upon Himself and to shed His blood (to die) for our sins.

At the cross, Jesus accomplished His goal in life. Just before Jesus died, He called out to heaven with the words which will ring in the ears of heaven and earth for all of eternity. Jesus accomplished what He came to do. Jesus did what only He as God's son could do. He died for us. Just before His death, Jesus said these words, "It is finished."

The finished work of Christ is the most important accomplished goal of all time. May we never forget what He did for us. May we never treat His life, His death and His resurrection flippantly. May we always be thankful and commit to doing the work which He has prepared for us to do. Are you looking for what He wants you to do? Are you being all that He wants you to be? Are you doing what He wants you to do? You have what it takes. You have been blessed with every spiritual blessing available. You have it and I have it so let's go. Let's look for what needs to be done and go do it. We need to say this as well. "This task that the Lord has given me is finished." Then go onto the next until He calls you home. I will be praying for all of you who are reading this today. I am pulling for you to be the man or woman which God Almighty would have you be.

Scripture reading: Ephesians 4:11-13, Romans 12:6-8, 1Corinthians 12:11

Draw near to God and He will draw near to you.

The Lord is Faithful

Many months ago, I issued a challenge to some college guys at Wake Forest University. Many of you reading this were some of those guys. I challenged them to walk with their God for 100 straight days. Since many of them did not have a daily devotional plan, I decided to write them a devotional each day. This collection is 72 of those devotionals, most of which came from that 100 day challenge. These devotions were written from everyday experiences or bible studies which I lead with the guys. As I walked with my Creator and looked for his presence in my life, I could not miss and wrote about the fact that the Lord is continuously active and involved in the world, my world and your world. I do hope that the journey of reading these devotionals was spiritually uplifting for the guys and has been encouraging to you all as well. My hope now is that these devotionals are read by others desiring to grow in their walk with our Lord.

Whether they know it or not, those young men will always be the ones to which those devotionals were originally sent and hopefully read. Those young men, in their college years with choices standing on every corner of their life, will be those who I was thinking about. As you know, my heart longs for those guys and every person created in the image of God to begin and grow in their walk with the Lord. Because of this opportunity to share my life and thoughts through these daily devotions, I just want to say thank you to everyone who has prayed and supported this endeavor and others like it. You will always be one of the band of supporters who encouraged and prayed for this life changing journey. I will be forever thankful for your partnership.

As you know, I want you all to be successful in life. I want you to find a fulfilling place in life where you will have time enough to achieve wonderful things and make an impact in the lives of those who are less fortunate. However, more than these very noble things, please know that I will want one thing more than anything else in your life. I will want you and will be praying for you to love the Lord your God with all of your heart, with all of your mind, with all of your soul and with all of your strength all the days of your life. And then, I will want you to love your neighbor as yourself. I implore you all to walk daily with your God, moment by moment checking in with His thoughts, His wisdom and His direction for your life. Never try to just think life through when you have the author of creation at your fingertips.

One of my favorite verses in all of the bible which reminds me and challenges me to learn of His ways constantly is Colossians 3:16. "Let the Word of Christ dwell in you richly as you teach and admonish one another with all wisdom, and as you sing psalms, hymns and spiritual songs with gratitude in your hearts to God."

Continue to seek after the truth. Continue to let the word of Christ (the truth) dwell in you richly. Find a bible study to stay engaged with. Look for a teacher who will challenge you to grow in your walk with the Lord. Find a fellowship of believers who desire to know the truth, learn the truth and walk humbly with their God. Also, do not be afraid to share your faith with others. For in so doing, the Lord will smile from on high, knowing that His coming to earth is being communicated to His world who desperately needs His forgiveness of sin and promise of a new life.

Three men went on separate journeys and became thirsty after a long walk. One came to a river and it was dry with no water in it. The other came to a river but the water was polluted. The final one came to a river and it was flowing with pure life giving water. Some paths will only lead you to a dry and hollow river bed. Other paths will lead you to statements and philosophies polluted with falsehood and deception. However, there is a river from which you can draw life giving water for your entire life. It is the river of life. This river of life is a person. Jesus Christ is the river of life. Jesus said "I am the way, the truth, and the life. No man comes to the Father but by Me." Go to Jesus every day and drink of His truth and His life. You will never regret that you did.

As always, draw near to God and He will draw near to you.